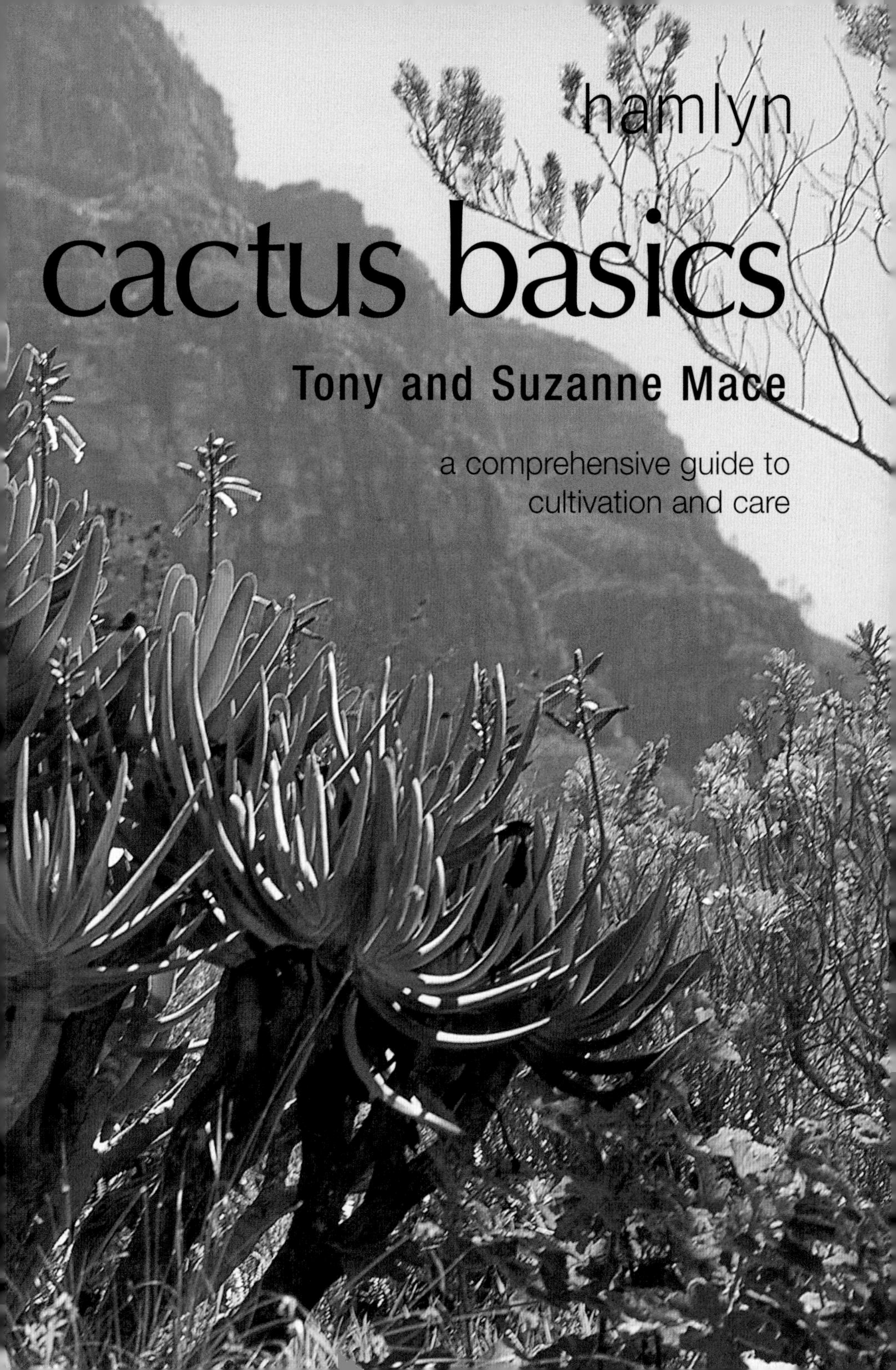

hamlyn

cactus basics

Tony and Suzanne Mace

a comprehensive guide to cultivation and care

A Pyramid Paperback

First published in Great Britain in 2006 by Hamlyn, a division of Octopus Publishing Group Ltd 2–4 Heron Quays, London E14 4JP

This material was previously published as *Cactus and Succulents*

Distributed in the United States and Canada by Sterling Publishing Co., Inc., 387 Park Avenue South, New York, NY 10016–8810

ISBN-13: 978-0-600-61468-5
ISBN-10: 0-600-61468-9

A CIP catalogue record for this book is available from the British Library

Printed and bound in China

10 9 8 7 6 5 4 3 2 1

Contents

Introduction

Introduction

The exotic nature of these unusual plants includes their vividly coloured, often extraordinary, flowers, which are one of their most desirable features.

Then there is the appeal of the strangely beautiful forms, from the numerous gem-like beauties to the intriguingly grotesque. The many bizarre shapes range from a claret cup to a barrel, a sea-urchin to a shark's jaw; a donkey's ear to a bird; some look for all the world like 'flowering stones', a perfect camouflage in their native habitat.

The convolutions, bearded woolliness and even the threat of strange and fierce spines bring a dimension not seen in other plants. Adding to their fascination, cacti and succulents originate in exotic parts of the world. They are notable for using their clever adaptations to withstand great extremes of temperature in some of the most remote and arid places on earth.

The novelty of these features has always attracted young enthusiasts to collecting cacti and succulents. Equally important, many of these plants are easy to care for and have a forgiving nature. Others present a great, but not impossible, challenge to the more experienced collector.

Dr Tony Mace and Suzanne Mace

Right: *Morangaya pensilis* **is an unusual cactus native to the tip of the Baya peninsula in California**

What are Cacti and Succulents?

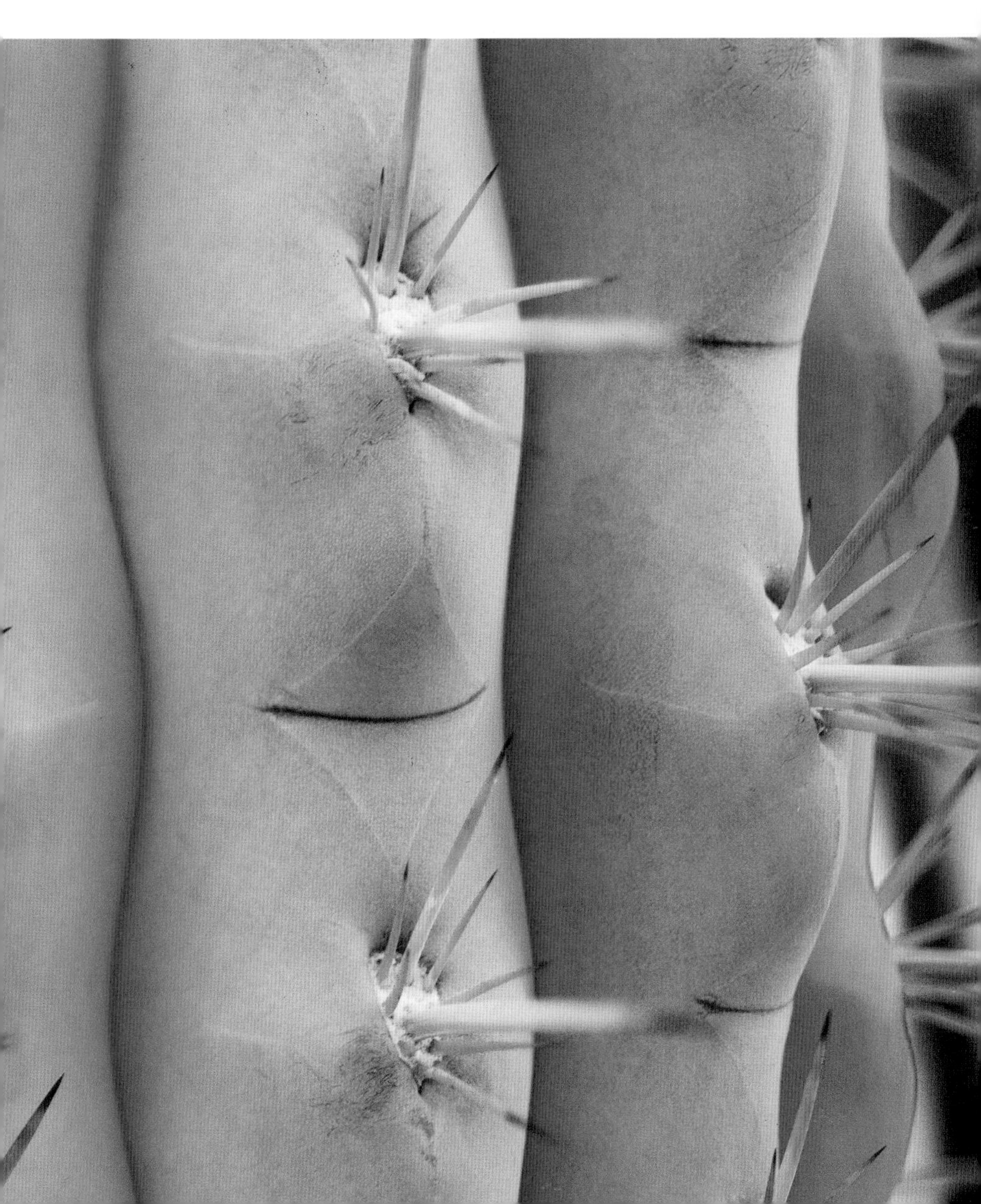

What are Cacti and Succulents?

Succulent plants, of which cacti are but one family, have developed ways of storing water so that, in a period of temporary water shortage, they are able to draw on their reserves, unlike many ordinary plants, which will wilt and die.

Their often strange appearance is a result of the modifications they have evolved to enable them to store water: thickened stems, leaves or roots. Other modifications either facilitate this storage of water or, equally importantly, reduce its loss. Cells of succulent plants are able to survive a greater variation in their water content than are the cells of ordinary plants. They frequently have a thickened epidermis or one covered in hairs or a waxy coating, which reduces water loss. The dense covering of spines plays a role in reducing the effect of intense solar heat on the plants by providing a partial shading effect.

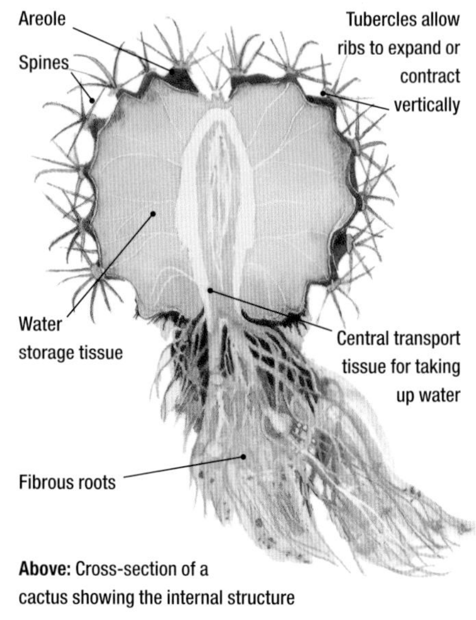

Above: Cross-section of a cactus showing the internal structure

Biochemical differences

One modification in succulent plants occurs at a less obvious biochemical level, and it operates in a way that is very different from the chemistry of most plants.

Plants produce food by photosynthesis, combining carbon dioxide and water to make sugars and starches, releasing oxygen in the process. The water is absorbed largely through the roots, while the carbon dioxide is taken in through minute apertures, called stomata, in the leaves. This occurs during daylight when the energy of sunlight drives the process. At the same time a lot of water evaporates through the leaves; this does not matter for ordinary plants because there is plenty of water available to replace the loss.

In the case of succulent plants, many have developed a modified process that enables them to keep their stomata closed during the day and to open them only at night. The photosynthetic process in these plants is called Crassulacean Acid Metabolism (CAM). Here, carbon dioxide is absorbed at night rather than during the day and is also combined into various organic acids. During the day this acid is turned into sugars by the action of photosynthesis. Interestingly, this phenomenon was known to ancient apothecaries: they realized that the taste of succulent plants varied greatly with the time of day they were collected, and this was due to the changing acid content.

This modified photosynthetic process has one very important effect for cultivators of succulents: it works best when there is a considerable difference between day-time and night-time temperatures. Succulents thrive, therefore, where there are certain extremes of temperature. This explains why many growers in tropical countries with high night-time temperatures find some succulents quite difficult to grow, when conditions otherwise appear to be ideal.

Where are cacti and succulents found?

The Cactaceae are a New World family. Their native habitats are found all the way from southern Canada down to Patagonia, but their peak distribution is in Mexico and some of the South American Andean countries. Cacti have been introduced into many other dry areas of the world where some have multiplied very rapidly and become seriously invasive – in Australia, for example.

Succulent plants are found in many areas of the world, but the largest concentrations are in Mexico and South America, particularly the Andean countries. Significant numbers occur in many South and Central American countries, as well as in East Africa, Arabia, Madagascar and India. Many small islands, such as the Canary Islands, also have a unique indigenous succulent flora. Interestingly, the deserts of Australia have few succulents (other than cacti), possibly because the period between rains is too long and unreliable.

Succulent Plant Families

Succulence occurs in many families of plants. One of the most familiar is the cactus family (Cactaceae). The term 'cacti and succulents' is strictly incorrect as cacti are already included in the word succulent. Virtually all cacti are succulent, although a few of the primitive ones have large, not very succulent leaves and can photosynthesize in the normal way. Cacti are distinguished from other plant families primarily by their flower and seed structure.

The easiest way to identify whether a plant is a cactus is to look for a structure called the areole. This is a growth point from which new offsets, flowers and spines arise. It varies in size from species to species but frequently displays at least a small amount of wool or small hairs. (Some other succulent plants, such

Below: A variety of growth forms for succulents

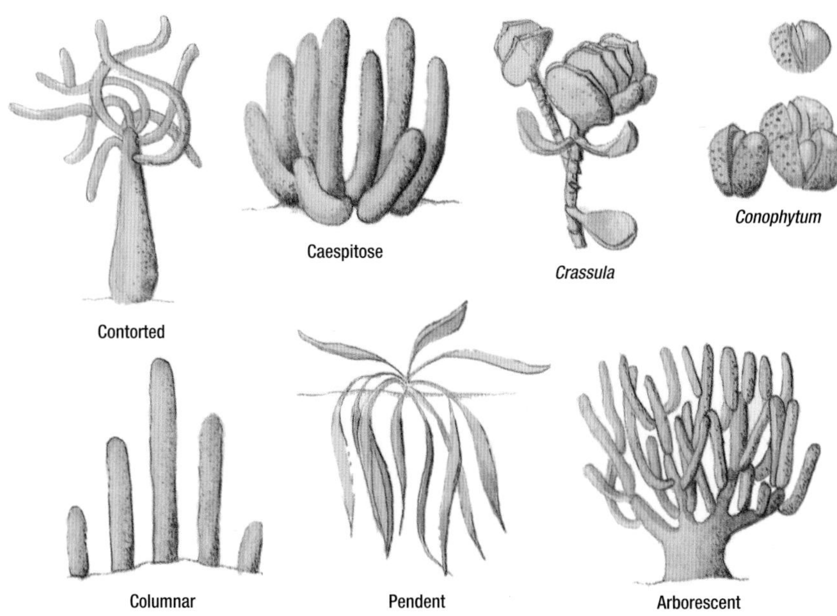

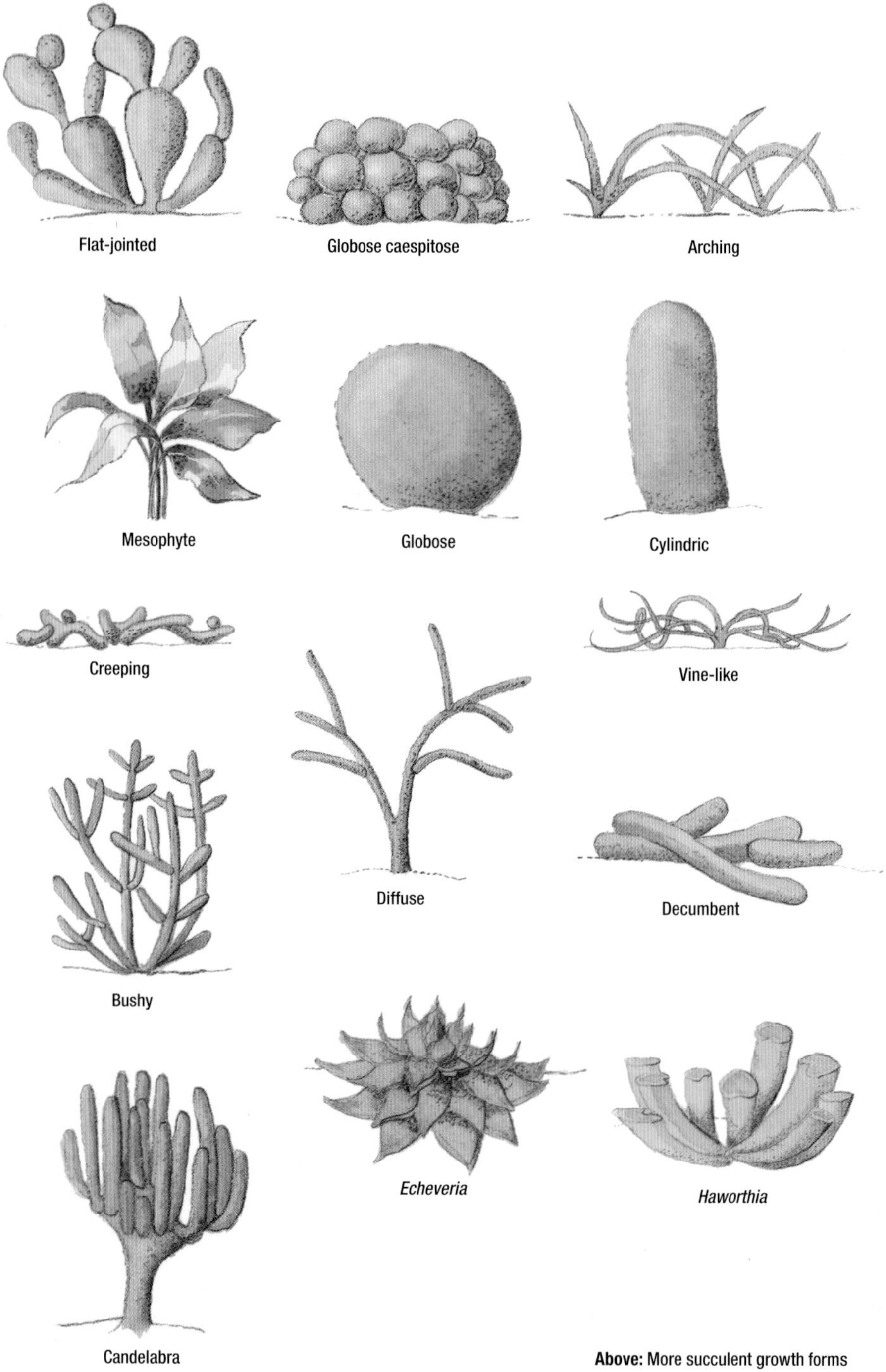

Flat-jointed

Globose caespitose

Arching

Mesophyte

Globose

Cylindric

Creeping

Vine-like

Diffuse

Decumbent

Bushy

Echeveria

Haworthia

Candelabra

Above: More succulent growth forms

as euphorbias, have spines but do not have the areole.) Other families have significant numbers of succulent species but may also have non-succulent ones. Typical examples are Euphorbiaceae and Asphodelaceae.

At least 2,000 species of cacti and 20,000 species of succulents occur in other plant families. Only a small fraction of these plants is discussed in this book, but some are included from the Agavaceae, Aizoaceae, Apocynaceae, Asclepadiaceae, Asphodelaceae, Asteraceae, Cactaceae, Crassulaceae, Dracenaceae and Euphorbiaceae families.

Above: ***Aloe plicatilis*****, an unusual aloe from South Africa, will eventually form a small bush**

Growth Forms

Cristate Plants

This phenomenon occurs when the growing point of a plant repeatedly divides, forming a continuous line of growth rather than the more normal single point. Such 'witches brooms' are known in a number of plant families, but are quite a common occurrence among cacti and some other groups of succulent plants.

As the fan of growth expands it forms a convoluted mass. Some collectors specialize in these forms and seek out rare new forms.

Below: ***Opuntia chlorotica*** **in its natural habitat – the Sonoran Desert**

There is a tendency for the ends of the fan to be pushed down into the soil, which makes the plant vulnerable to rots, so it is not uncommon for them to be grafted onto a taller cactus in order to keep the growing point away from damp soil.

What causes this growth form to occur in the first place is not certain. It is probably not an inherited characteristic and such plants are usually propagated by cuttings or by grafting. Cristate plants are usually extremely reluctant to flower.

Monstrose Plants

These plants are similar to cristate plants, but the growth points separate before dividing again. This results in plants with many growth points. This occurs mostly in a few species of *Cereus*. Another variant on this theme occurs on some species of *Opuntia*, where every areole produces a shoot resulting in masses of tiny offsets. Still other rib-and-spine arrangements occur, such as the monstrose form of *Lophocereus schottii*, which is almost completely spineless.

Why Grow Cacti and Succulents?

There is a fascination in watching any plant grow as it matures and becomes an object of beauty. When it comes to growing cacti and succulents there is a particular appeal on several levels.

Above: *Dudleya pachyphytum*, a choice species from an island off the coast of California

Find a daily source of wonder

Their exotic nature, often unusual colours and forms and very beautiful flowers can be a constant source of wonderment and enjoyment.

Your curiosity is stimulated, then your questions are answered as a plant grows and changes in your care, and you begin to understand how and why it responds in a certain way, the way that is natural for it.

Meet the challenge

The requirements of growing these exotic plants set them apart. Their cultivation in unfavourable climates presents some challenges to be overcome.

Below: The species *Mammillaria multidigita* tends to form clumps

However, it is quite possible to grow them successfully, and you can to your great personal satisfaction.

Enjoy the anticipation

Slow-growing cacti and succulents may take many years to become fully mature. This characteristic is shared by only a relatively few groups of plants: bonsai trees and some alpines come to mind.

For those with patience, it is so exciting when for the first time a cactus plant, which you may have looked after for 30 years, finally produces a magnificent flower.

Grow plants well suited to modern living

Practical considerations make cacti and succulents especially suitable plants for cultivation in modern homes. You can leave cacti and succulents for a few weeks while you go on holiday without making arrangements for them to be watered. On your return, they will not be wilting or dead, like most other plants.

Also, if space is limited it is quite possible to grow a very large number of cacti and succulent species. All that is needed is careful selection of miniature species and forms. You will be spoiled for choice.

Focus on one aspect

Like people with other multi-faceted interests, cacti and succulent enthusiasts derive pleasure from focusing on specific aspects of the subject. Some people become interested in seed raising and propagation; others specialize in a particular group of plants; while still others become avid exhibitors, endeavouring to grow the finest specimens in order to win trophies.

'New eyes' through travel

For those who travel, it is fascinating and educational to visit the areas where cacti and succulents grow naturally. A new depth of understanding is to be gained from seeing the plants in their native habitats. It may even be possible to search for rare species in habitat. Remember, most countries have severe restrictions on removing plants and plant material from the wild to help conserve the plants in their habitats. Of course, there are no restrictions on photographing these plants in their spectacular natural settings. Organized field trips are readily available in North America and South Africa.

People all over the world are interested in these plants and they are usually only too happy to meet, or communicate with, other lovers of cacti and succulents to discuss their favourite plants. This is a source of contacts and friends worldwide.

Join a local group

On a local level, groups meet regularly to discuss the various aspects of collecting cacti and succulents. Here is a valuable and close-to-home source of information and help for you.

Among the activities, guest speakers may be invited to entertain and educate. Local mini-shows are also sometimes arranged.

Outings and open days enable the group to visit cactus nurseries, or even other growers' collections to see how their plants are doing. Joining in with all these activities gives you good feedback, which you can relate to your own plants regarding their appearance or unusual behaviour.

In the group, you can easily, often cheaply, increase your collection. Collectors bring reasonably priced plants and other items for sale at these meetings.

Many of the plants are so long lived that they are often passed on from collector to collector. The original owner may have stopped keeping plants through old age, or the plant may have become too big to manage, either too heavy or too tall. But what do you do with a plant that is too big? You will derive your own pleasure from growing and caring for these strangely beautiful living things. Cacti and succulents have a special place in the affections of thousands of collectors, and this book will give you practical advice and guidance so you too can achieve success with these plants.

Below: ***Aloe arborescens*****, which is native to southern Africa, is one of the tallest species**

Cultivation

Cultivation

The largest single mistake that is made by inexperienced growers of cacti and succulents is to forget that they are plants and therefore have similar requirements to other plants: water, food, air and light. Cacti and succulents are adapted to fairly extreme conditions, but they cannot thrive without these vital elements.

No cacti or succulents grow in a true desert consisting only of sand and where there is no rainfall. Most grow in what is usually described as semi-desert, where rainfall occurs for a limited number of months in the year and other xerophytic shrubs and annual plants are common. Many small cacti and succulents begin life in the shade of these bushes, growing above them only when they are large and relatively robust.

The soil in such places is usually relatively poor in humus but often rich in mineral nutrients, needing only sufficient water to turn it into a fertile medium. Many cacti and succulents can grow in wetter areas than their natural habitat, but they are less efficient than their more leafy counterparts and so lose out to the competition.

Many features of cacti and succulents are adapted to absorb and store water from the rainfall when it is present so that the plants can survive through the dry season. These features include a ribbed stem structure to allow for expansion and contraction and a widespread root system for the rapid uptake of water.

Where to Grow?

Cacti and succulent plants are extremely popular horticultural subjects and are grown in many countries over an enormous range of climatic conditions. There are collectors growing them in places as far apart as Alaska and Singapore.

Indoors

If you have a small number of plants it is possible to grow them indoors. Some groups of succulents adapt much more easily to these conditions than others. The range of plants that can be grown successfully indoors is increased considerably if artificial lighting is used (see page 28). This may be the method you choose if you live in an area with extreme winter weather where it is not economic to maintain a frost-free greenhouse.

Greenhouse or conservatory

In climates where winter temperatures rarely fall below -10°C (14°F), a freestanding greenhouse or conservatory is probably the best choice. The use of cellular plastic materials, such as double- or triple-walled polycarbonate, a much better insulator than glass, has extended the practical range of such structures (see also page 29). A variant on this idea is the use of heated frames, which can be very effective for globular cacti. A limited range of succulent plants can survive unprotected in these climates and so can be grown outside. The range of such hardy plants may be greater in very dry areas or if protection from the wet is given in an unheated alpine-style house.

Outside

In favourable climates, where frost is rare, a wide range of succulents can be grown outside. If the amount of rain is particularly heavy, it may be necessary either to modify the soil so it is especially free draining or to provide protection in the form of a lath house. The latter can also be useful in more tropical areas to provide some protection from the sun for those species accustomed to growing under bushes or in more shady areas.

Right: A collection of cacti and succulents growing on a sunny windowsill

Containers

Cacti and succulents can be grown in a wide range of containers and will do well in most. Always bear in mind the eventual size and shape of the plant. We are dealing with a vast range, from miniature plants, which will never exceed 1.25 cm (½ in) in diameter, to plants that can grow to 12 m (40 ft) tall and weigh many tons.

Small plastic or ceramic pots

Smaller plants, which grow naturally in rock crevices, are more successful when grown in small pots, which may be plastic or ceramic.

Shallow pans

Large clumping plants may prefer shallower pans, which will allow them to spread sideways.

Long toms

Plants that develop long taproots may be better suited to long toms. Long-tom pots, which are very deep, are sometimes referred to as rose pots by garden centres.

Left: Clay pots are suitable for cacti and succulents

Below: A globular *Ferocactus chrysacanthus* in a clay pot

Above: A collection of cacti and succulents in containers as they might appear in a conservatory or on a patio

Full-depth pots

Larger growing plants need full-depth pots and fairly regular repotting for optimum growth. Some of the larger plants respond quite spectacularly to being grown with a free root run.

Drainage

It is much safer for those people who are inexperienced in growing cacti and succulents to grow them in containers with one or more drainage holes. Without the drainage hole, watering must be exactly correct. It is also important to remember that larger containers take much longer to dry out after watering than smaller containers, and of course this has implications for the soil and watering (see page 25).

Some species of cacti and succulents – those that naturally occur in very arid regions – are particularly sensitive to their roots becoming waterlogged for too long. It is best to grow these plants in porous clay containers, which will dry out more quickly. Remember, the larger the container you are using, the more important this is.

Soil

The type of soil that is suitable for cacti and succulents is a source of endless debate: there are almost as many soil recipes as there are growers. Many growers have used different types over the years and found it possible to grow good plants, particularly of the easier species, in many types of growing medium. Many cacti and succulents are rather long-lived, slow-growing plants and may therefore easily be kept in the same container with the same compost for a considerable period of time.

Function of the soil

The growing medium is not only a source of moisture and nutrients but also provides mechanical support for the plants.

Peat-based composts

Plants from garden centres and other wholesale sources are frequently grown in peat-based mixtures. The reason for this is partly because young plants grow quickly in this medium and partly because the soil is light for transport and simplifies mechanical handling at the nursery. The slightly acid reaction of the soil is particularly suitable for some South American cacti such as *Notocactus* and *Gymnocalycium*.

The food in such composts is used up rapidly so it is important to use a soluble feed at regular intervals. The feed should be high in potash and phosphorus and low in nitrogen. A high nitrogen feed will encourage plants to put on rather soft growth, leading to a susceptibility to pests and diseases and encouraging vegetative growth at the expense of flowering.

Peat-based soils are particularly suitable for epiphytic cacti such as the *Epiphyllums* and the Christmas cactus (*Schlumbergera*). Some growers report good results with adding water-retaining gel crystals, which are available from garden centres and from hardware stores.

When plants are not watered frequently the use of peat-based soils can lead to problems. The first difficulty arises when a peat-based soil completely dries out, for it can be difficult to re-wet. This can be overcome to some degree by adding a small amount of a wetting agent, such as a detergent, to the first watering after the rest period. The second difficulty occurs after a period of a few years when the peat tends to break down, resulting in a change in the soil structure. It is believed that this breakdown produces chemicals that have a damaging effect on the roots of certain species of cacti, particularly those from drier areas, which are often regarded as more difficult to grow. To combat this effect, plants in peat-based composts need to be repotted fairly regularly.

Many gardeners prefer to avoid peat-based products because of the damage extraction causes to the environment. There are many suitable alternatives.

Soil-based composts

Many growers use various types of proprietary soil-based composts. In some areas John Innes formulation composts are available. They are frequently mixed with coarse sand or gravel to produce a free-draining mix. The key to a good compost is to provide one that has a large capacity for absorbing water and chemical nutrients without becoming waterlogged. Materials with very high porosity, such as ground pumice, are widely used in areas of the USA where it is available. In Europe artificial substitutes, such as perlite, have been used with considerable success.

Most soil-based composts contain a fertilizer that will last longer than that of a peat-based compost, perhaps up to six months, but they will eventually require additional feeding. Good results can be achieved with granular slow-release fertilizers added to the compost. Slow-release fertilizers remain active for longer in cactus and succulent soils as the plants do not absorb the food as quickly as garden annuals, partly because they do not grow as fast and are not watered so frequently or heavily. They may continue to provide food for up to 18 months. Depending on the sources of materials, plants kept in the same containers for many years may well become deficient in some trace elements. This may show up as chlorosis or as weak, poor or distorted growth. Occasional use of a fertilizer containing trace elements should prevent this from happening.

Some succulents, such as mesembryanthemums, are used to a fine-grained, almost clay-like, fairly compacted soil in their native habitat. In cultivation these plants do not grow well in loose peat-based composts, preferring a finer-grained soil-based one.

Hydroponic systems

Surprisingly, a few growers have been successful with growing cacti in a hydroponic system. There are technical difficulties, in part arising from the mechanical support needed by heavy plants, and such experiments should be undertaken only after advice from someone with experience of this form of cultivation.

Above: Xerophytic cacti very quickly show signs of water stress

Watering

One of the most frequently asked questions and one of the most difficult to answer, is: when should I water my plants? Because cacti and succulents do not wilt like other plants there is no visual automatic indicator. Also, because there are so many variables, such as temperature, size of pot, type of soil, rapidity of plant growth and type of plant, there can be no easy formula such as 'once a week' or 'once a month'.

In general, these plants will do best if they are left almost to dry out completely between waterings. This might be daily for plants in small

Below: Three methods of watering cacti and succulents

Above: Overwatering will result in splitting or, worse, rotting

pots in a hot greenhouse that are growing well. But large plants in big pots in cooler weather may need watering only once every three or four weeks. This is why a well-drained, open compost is so important: it leaves a much wider margin for error in watering.

Points to consider when watering

- Small pots dry out faster than large ones.
- Unglazed ceramic pots dry out more quickly than plastic or glazed ones.
- Plants in active growth use more water than those that are not growing.
- Plants grown in areas where the climate is hot and humidity low dry out more quickly than those in a cool, humid climate. (This includes plants grown in centrally heated environments.)
- Succulents with a large leaf area use more water than species without leaves.
- Most cacti and succulents are accustomed to a long dormant spell. In most cases this corresponds to our colder, darker winter period, but plants from the southern hemisphere will not change their growing season, growing during the northern hemisphere winter.
- Plants stop growing if they are short of water but may rot if overwatered. If in doubt, it is safer to err on the side of underwatering. If small pots dry out quickly, it may be useful to plunge them on a gravel tray.
- If pots are staying too wet for too long, it may be necessary to apply more artificial heat. This decreases the relative humidity and stimulates water uptake by the plants.

Some growers water their plants carefully, making sure that no water gets on to the stem. While this might be important under poor growing conditions, it is not necessary when plants are in full growth. From time to time a hose can be used in the greenhouse to give everything a thorough drenching. This also has the merit of removing dust and cobwebs. Mist spraying of some species can also be beneficial; indeed some genera, such as the genus *Copiapoa*, obtain most of their moisture from coastal mists in their native habitats in Chile.

Repotting

When to repot

Soil in a pot will eventually become exhausted and needs to be replaced. A plant may have outgrown its container and require a larger one. If you suspect that something is wrong with a plant, repot it to have a good look at its roots in search of the problem.

Handling cacti

Handling cacti can be tricky. Many people find the wearing of gloves useless: they rapidly become full of spines and can be as uncomfortable as the cactus itself.

Handling tips

- Hold young plants at the neck where the spines are weak or non-existent.
- Hold the plant by its rootball, if it is strong.
- Hold plants with fewer, stronger spines between the spines or by the spines if possible.
- It may be possible to hold plants with many uniform spines with little discomfort as the pressure is distributed over many points (the fakir's-bed principle).
- Manipulate tall plants with a temporary strap made of newspaper, which is then disposable.
- Use broad wooden tongs.
- Wrap very large, heavy, spiny plants in sheets of expanded polystyrene.

Succulents, with the exception of a few, such as euphorbias, are less problematic.

Watch out for

- Hooked spined plants – it is possible to get badly entangled in them.
- The genus *Opuntia* and relatives, whose barbed spines (glochids) are difficult to remove. The best way to remove them is to apply transparent adhesive tape to your skin (where the spines are stuck in). When the tape is pulled off, it will remove the majority of these irritant spines.
- The sap of euphorbias can be inflammatory in cuts or other sensitive skin areas. If affected, wash immediately with cold water and seek medical advice.

Below: 1. A mammillaria in a 9 cm (3½ in) pot desperately needing to be repotted **2.** Tip out the plant onto your palm or a wad of newspaper, examining the roots for any problems, such as insects or damage **3.** Select a slightly larger pot (about 2.5 cm/1 in in diameter larger), cover the bottom with drainage material (broken clay pot shards), put a little of the new compost in the pot, place the plant in position and fill gaps with new soil **4.** Finally, topdress with fine aquarium gravel. Do not water for at least one week after repotting

Above: Poor light results in pale, drawn growth, weak spines and lack of flowers

Indoor Cultivation

Some plants take particularly well to indoor cultivation. They may indeed grow better than they do in a greenhouse. Epiphytic cacti are a good example of this, as are hoyas, ceropegias and sansevierias. Many other plants will grow as well as they will in a greenhouse. These include plants of the genera *Rebutia, Notocactus* and *Gymnocalycium*, some mammillarias, aloes, haworthias, stapeliads and some crassulas. Some of the leafy euphorbias are also quite at home indoors.

In countries with severe winters there may be no option but to keep plants indoors. In eastern Europe many collectors use their greenhouses only in summer, because heating greenhouses is expensive or impracticable. In winter they remove the plants from the pots and store them, wrapped in newspaper, in a cool, dry cellar – a surprisingly successful technique.

Artificial lighting

The use of artificial lighting makes it possible to grow almost any succulent plant indoors, with the possible exception of some of the taller growing species because they are difficult to accommodate and light adequately.

A book could be written about artificial lighting for plants, but a few basics need to be mentioned. Plants make use of light at particular frequencies, and these must be provided by the artificial lighting you use.

Tungsten bulbs The normal incandescent tungsten bulb provides little light of the right frequency and is more or less useless from the point of view of the plant.

Fluorescent tubes The most commonly used lights for plants are fluorescent tubes. Many types are available, but some have been designed to emit the right colours for plants. Largely developed for the aquarium business, they are also the best type to use for succulents. They are fairly cheap to run, but the fluorescent material on the inside of the glass tube starts deteriorating fairly quickly after six months' use, so tubes must be replaced regularly.

To provide sufficient lighting for succulent plants use closely spaced tubes. It helps to have good reflectors so that the maximum amount of light is directed towards the plants. Check the amount of heat generated from the tube ballasts or starters to make sure the temperature does not become excessive. If the fluorescent tubes are kept on a time-switch to control the day length rather than operated manually, you may need a special circuit breaker as the tubes create a current surge when switched on.

Metal halide lamps These can be used for plants requiring additional daylight length. Commercial growers prefer them as they produce more light for the same amount of energy. The equipment needed to run them is expensive, as are the lamps, but if you have a large set-up, they are worth investigating.

Watering

Indoor environments are warmer and drier than a greenhouse or some conservatories so the plants may need occasional watering in winter.

Greenhouse and Conservatory Cultivation

Greenhouses and conservatories, with their strong light and abundant warmth, suit many cacti and succulents.

Heated Greenhouses

A greenhouse is in many ways the best place to grow cacti and succulents because it is designed to give maximum control over the environment. Carefully selecting, siting and constructing your greenhouse will ensure success in growing cacti and succulents in it.

Size

Most collectors have a very small greenhouse, 3 x 2 m (8 x 6 ft), and this can present particular problems, such as overheating, and lack of air movement. Modern gardens, particularly in Europe, tend to be quite small, which may not leave space for anything larger; however, it is possible to have a very interesting collection in a small area. If space is at a premium, choose plants that are going to stay small. Many species of cacti and succulent rarely exceed 8 cm (3 in) in diameter.

Site

Selecting the site for your greenhouse, preferably before you buy it, is obviously important. Remember that greenhouses that are sited with the ridge running east–west receive more light than those with the ridge running north–south.

Base and floor

The base and floor of your greenhouse are very important. Concrete is best, as it helps to keep

Above: **Cacti and succulents in a typical greenhouse, with aluminium staging and a concrete floor. Adequate light, heat and ventilation are very important**

the moisture down and the light intensity up. Rest the structure on, and secure it to, a course or two of bricks. A dark earth floor will attract moisture, slugs and snails, moles, mice and other soil-borne pests and diseases. Putting paving slabs down is an easier alternative to installing a permanent concrete floor, but will still allow many outsiders in.

Staging the plants

Once the size of the structure is decided, it is equally important to think about arrangements for staging the plants. Different levels of shelves will enable you to place plants with different requirements appropriately to allow them to thrive.

Try to arrange all plants in reachable positions, so a number of other plants will not have to be moved to get to them. When you have run out of space, put up a few hanging shelves to relieve the burden.

We remember once seeing a collection of cacti in a greenhouse, but were unable to work out where one could walk inside to see the plants. Every part of the floor had staging on it. How did the owner get at them? Did he take the glass out? It transpired that the final, lowest level of very short plants were on trolleys, which were pushed under the benching as he entered the greenhouse, and pulled out again upon leaving!

Ventilation

If the greenhouse is fairly small, ventilation is going to be critical as a small structure heats up extremely quickly.

Normal greenhouses are sold with too little ventilation for cacti and succulents. Consider adding extra windows or louvre vents. An electric extractor fan could also be a very useful addition.

It is best not to let a greenhouse go over 40°C (105°F) for any length of time, because this makes the plants go dormant even if it does not damage them. You can usually keep to this by providing enough natural ventilation and the occasional use of forced electric-fan ventilation. If your summers are particularly hot, it may be necessary to provide shading.

Heating

Most growers will require some form of heating for their cacti and succulents.

Electric heaters This is by far the easiest form to use. Quite accurate thermostatic controls are available and these will minimize the cost. Unlike gas or paraffin (kerosene) heating, no additional water is added to the atmosphere.

Gas or paraffin heaters If this method is used, there must be some ventilation at all times to provide sufficient oxygen.

Paraffin (or kerosene) heaters When allowed to burn with inadequate air, these can produce a smoky flame, which can make a terrible mess of the plants. You must make additional water

Above: Cactus showing damage caused by cold

available in the atmosphere. Also, some leafy succulents may be sensitive to sulphurous compounds in the gas supply.

Under-soil heating cables If you are growing a small number of more tender succulents, propagators incorporating under-soil heating cables can be a useful facility.

Insulation

Insulation is particularly important for smaller greenhouses. Larger structures are naturally much more stable in temperature, taking longer to heat up and cool down, and in many ways are therefore easier to manage.

Bubble-wrap plastic Many growers line their greenhouses with bubble-wrap plastic to add additional insulation. This can be a useful short-term solution, but the disadvantages outweigh the advantages: it considerably reduces the ventilation and light and tends to hold condensation inside the greenhouse. If it is used, choose a horticultural grade of plastic, which is not so rapidly degraded by UV light.

Polycarbonate sheeting If you live in an area that has extremely severe winters you should consider replacing the glass with twin- or even triple-wall polycarbonate sheeting. Although the thicker grades of this material are quite expensive, it is quite durable and the savings in heating costs will almost certainly outweigh the expense of installation.

Conservatories

Many people have the ideal place in which to grow cacti and succulents: a sun-room or conservatory attached to the house. These plants are perfect for sun-rooms and conservatories, which are very often too hot and dry for most other plants.

A difficulty is that such structures often have inadequate or no ventilation. This can be avoided if the structure is designed from scratch, but if you are adapting an existing structure the simplest solution is to install an extractor fan or two.

In a conservatory it is worthwhile having a bench that will allow you to plunge the pots into a coarse, granular, water-retaining material. Such materials are available from DIY stores and garden centres and are frequently used for other types of plants as well.

Create natural-looking planted beds within your conservatory, so that large plants can grow and develop attractively.

If children or animals are likely to use the area, it may be a good idea to restrict the plants you select to the less spiky and less dangerous succulents.

Cold Greenhouse

The range of plants that can be grown in a cold greenhouse is naturally somewhat restricted, compared to a structure in which some heat is used.

Succulent plants originating in East and West Africa, the Arabian peninsula, southern Mexico, the West Indies, Venezuela and Brazil should be avoided because they will not survive in temperatures below 7°C (45°F) for extended periods.

Some of the globular cacti, such as echinocereus and lobivias, are the best subjects for a cold greenhouse. Of the succulents, some species of agave are amongst the hardiest. *Agave americana*, for example, will tolerate temperatures as low as 5°C (41°F), although most species prefer a minimum of 10°C (50°F). Many South African plants will also withstand temperatures just below freezing for a short period.

Frames

This method of cultivation can be very effective for species that do not grow too tall. A frame, or cold frame, is a permanent or portable structure with a glazed top. Use a heating cable to maintain the required minimum temperature in winter, and make sure that the top of the frame can be removed in summer to give your plants maximum sun and air. The use of frames for cacti is more common in mainland Europe than in Britain or the USA.

Above: How the sun's rays affect a greenhouse

What is Hardiness?

Hardiness is the ability of a plant to withstand low temperatures or several degrees of frost in the open air.

Many cacti, including some succulents, can endure quite low temperatures in their natural environments. They may either originate in areas at extreme northern or southern latitudes or grow naturally at high altitudes. The plants from the extreme latitudes are more likely to prove hardy under most conditions as they are more used to prolonged periods of adverse weather conditions. The high-altitude plants experience extreme swings of conditions: very cold nights and intense solar heat during the day, as well as high light intensity. Changes in conditions such as these are not easy to simulate in cultivation. To avoid disappointment, remember that what is hardy under your own local conditions will vary considerably, depending not only on the minimum temperatures, but also on the rainfall, snow cover and winter sunshine that your local climate provides.

Hardy Plants

A few succulents are traditionally grown as hardy plants for they are tolerant of quite severe conditions.

Sempervivum

Sempervivums are alpine plants that, if given a well-drained soil, such as that used in a rock garden, will thrive. These attractive plants are deservedly popular, and a wide range of hybrids is also available.

However, a few species are not fully hardy and do need protection from very wet weather.

Below: ***Agave huachucensis*** **is native to Mexico and has beautiful blue leaves and very dark brown, almost black teeth and apical spine**

Above: ***Opuntia erinacea*** **has long, dense white spines, and there are varieties with pink or yellow flowers**

Sedum

Sedums are commonly grown as hardy plants. More care is needed with the selection of the species of this genus, because some of the species that are native to southern Mexico are definitely not hardy.

Yucca

Some species of yucca are frequently grown as hardy garden plants. There are several species (not commonly available in the horticultural trade), that would make perfectly hardy and interesting garden plants, but there are also quite a few species that, although they will withstand considerable cold, cannot be used as garden plants because they are sensitive to excess moisture: the classic example of this is the Joshua tree (*Yucca brevifolia*) of the Mohave Desert in Arizona. The yucca that is commonly sold as a house plant is definitely *not* hardy, except in the most favourable climates, as it comes from largely frost-free areas of Mexico. One of the factors holding back greater horticultural use of yuccas is the lack of good literature on the genus.

Agave

Some species of *Agave* are reasonably hardy, surviving -15°C (5°F) of frost even if wet. The most likely cause of damage is frequent freezing/thawing cycles of ice in the centres of the plants. If kept under drier shelter many could undoubtedly survive lower temperatures. A related plant, *Dasylirion wheeleri*, appears to be quite happy outside all year.

Opuntia

Quite a number of species of *Opuntia* are hardy, particularly the low-growing species from Canada and the northern USA, such as some forms of *Opuntia fragilis*, *O. polyacantha*, *O. humifusa* and *O. macrorhiza*. These make good rock-garden plants, producing attractive flower displays in spring. The spines and glochids make weeding difficult, but growers have found that opuntias are not particularly susceptible to the effects of selective weedkillers, so this is a possible method of solving this particular problem.

Other species of *Opuntia* are tolerant of very cold conditions but are somewhat more sensitive to excess moisture; *O. basilaris* and *O. erinacea* fall into this category.

Other hardy cacti

This sensitivity to excess moisture applies to most other hardy cacti. It includes a number of species of *Echinocereus*, such as *E. triglochidiatus*, some northerly occurring forms of *Escobaria vivipara*, *Neobesseya missouriensis* and *Pediocactus simpsonii*.

A number of the mesembryanthemums will tolerate fairly extreme low temperatures, but only if they are very dry.

Propagation

Seeds

Growing from seed is the largest single method of propagating cacti and succulents. Seed is available for a wide range of species and is inexpensive when purchased from specialist suppliers. Mixed packets of seed from general suppliers tend to be rather expensive, and the mixture of fast- and slow-growing types makes their cultivation more difficult.

Method

It is sensible to begin with the more robust, quickly growing species before progressing to those cacti and succulents that are fairly slow to get established and therefore need more care. Many growers have developed their own favourite methods, and it may be necessary for you to experiment a little to find out what works best for you.

Containers

Decide on the kinds of containers you are going to use. If you are growing large numbers of the same sort, a traditional rectangular seed pan is fine. This is suitable for up to 2,000 seeds. If, as is more likely, you have a packet of 20–30 seeds, use small pieces of plastic or glass to divide the tray into small squares for each sort. Alternatively, use small individual pots; small square ones are most convenient.

Below: Cactus fruit showing the seed embedded in a sweet pulp

Growing medium

Use the same compost as for bigger plants but pass it through a sieve to remove the larger particles. It is also important that the compost is prepared from clean materials that are free of weed seeds and fungi. It may be useful to sterilize it. After filling the containers, place them in a tray of water and allow the compost to become saturated.

Sowing seed

The seed should be thinly and evenly sprinkled on the surface of the compost. Cover the seeds with a thin layer of coarse grit. The seeds of Mesembryanthemaceae, such as lithops, need light to germinate and should not be covered.

Germination

Most seeds germinate best at around 21°C (70°F). It may be necessary to use some artificial heat to reach this temperature, particularly if the seeds are being started early in the year. A difference between day and night temperatures will improve germination. It is necessary to maintain a fairly humid atmosphere while the seeds are germinating. Either seal individual pots in plastic bags or cover trays with sheets of glass or plastic. Once the seedlings have germinated they can be introduced to the light and more air, although direct sunshine is not a good idea at this stage. Keep them reasonably moist and do not allow them to dry out completely.

When to start seedlings

Start seedlings fairly early in the year, so they have a reasonably long growing season before

their first winter. After six months, faster growing kinds, particularly some of the succulents, columnar cacti and opuntias, can be ready for pricking out into individual small pots or trays. Slower growing species can be left in their original containers for a year or more.

Reluctance to germinate

Some seeds can be reluctant to germinate. The seed coat may contain germination inhibitors or the seed must be a few years old before it will germinate. Alternatively, cold/heat cycles are needed to prepare the seed for germination.

Pests and diseases

Watering with a copper-fungicide solution may help prevent damping-off. Look out for small, black insects (Sciarid Fly, Mushroom Flies or Fungus Gnats see pages 45–46), whose grubs can rapidly destroy pans of seedlings.

Labelling

It is important to label seeds so the individual species can be identified. It may be simplest to give each container a numbered tag and maintain an index elsewhere.

Above: Pans of seedlings with young plants already flowering in their second year

Cuttings

Many cacti and succulents are readily propagated by cuttings. With non-succulent plants the chief problem is that cuttings wilt before they can form roots to absorb water. With cacti and succulents the main difficulty is fungal rots entering cut surfaces. It is important to keep any cut surfaces clean and allow them to form a dry callous over the wound before placing the cuttings in soil. The time this takes depends on the area of the cut surface and the temperature and humidity when the cuttings are taken. It is usually best to minimize the cut area by taking stem or shoot cuttings at a narrow point. The exception to this is epiphyllum cuttings, which root better from a broad cut on the stem. Allow one or two weeks before planting the cuttings in moist soil.

Large cuttings with a broad area of cut can be left for a month or more. Some cuttings that root slowly may benefit from gentle bottom heat. Stem cuttings of some leafy succulents can be planted almost immediately. Clumping cacti or spreading succulents may grow roots while still on the parent plants, and these can also be potted up much more quickly. For plants sensitive to rot, dusting the stems with fungicidal powder or flowers of sulphur can be useful. Hormone rooting powder is not usually necessary but may be helpful.

Above: Roots forming on a cactus cutting

Plants to propagate by cuttings

Most mesembryanthemums can be propagated from cuttings, even the succulent species such as lithops. However, it is important that a small amount of the woody tissue at the base of the leaves be included in the cutting. Single leaves may occasionally root but will not form a new growing point. Single leaves of some other succulents can be propagated in this way, including sansevierias, gasterias, some echeverias, sedums and pachyphytums. Even a part of a leaf of sansevierias and gasterias may root and produce plantlets. Take whole fresh leaves cleanly from the stem or in some cases from the inflorescence of echeverias.

Grafting

Grafting cacti, and to a lesser extent some succulents, is a useful technique and can be used for the following purposes: to grow difficult or weakly growing species by placing them on a vigorous rootstock; to keep cristate plants clear of the soil to avoid the danger of rotting; to force some species into the rapid proliferation of offsets, which can then be grafted again or rerooted on their own roots as cuttings. Grafting is also the only way of keeping alive the genetic aberrations of completely variegated plants.

Plant families to graft

It is important to remember that the technique works only with dicotyledons – plants with two seedling leaves. Monocotyleds, such as Asphodelaceae or Agavaceae, lack the internal structures that make success in grafting possible. Grafts are commonly used for Cactaceae and occasionally for Euphorbiaceae, Portulaceae, Asclepiadaceae and Apocynaceae.

Points to note

Grafts between plants of closely related species are more likely to be successful, and the more closely related, the more successful the graft will be. Indeed, plants of different families rarely make successful grafts.

Grafts are best undertaken when both the stock (the rooted part) and the scion (the top part) are in active growth, probably in the spring or summer. The stock and scion should be of similar diameter and turgidity.

Stock plants

Many species can be used as stock plants, but the genus *Trichocereus* is probably favourite. If *Echinopsis* is used it should not be a species that offsets too freely.

Commercial grafts are often done on three-ribbed *Hylocereus*, which is very vigorous, but its need for high winter temperatures causes problems for amateurs. Another stock with similar problems but not quite so demanding, is *Myrtillocactus geometrizans*, recognized by the slightly glaucous, six-angled stems.

Specialists in grafting tiny seedlings often recommend *Pereskiopsis*, which can

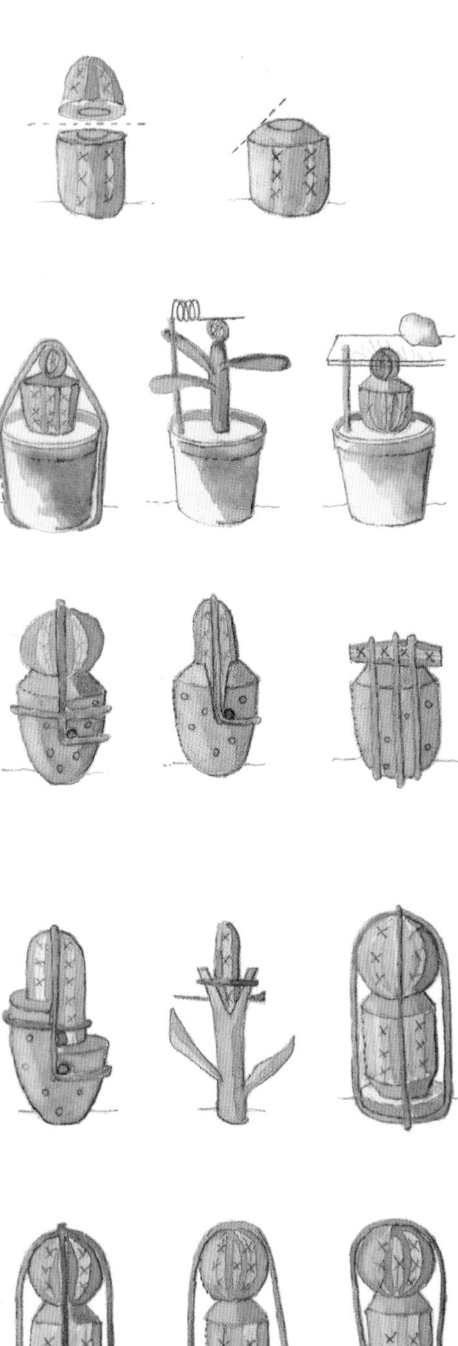

sometimes turn tiny seedlings into flowering plants in a matter of months. Very vigorous opuntias can sometimes be the best stock for grafting other opuntias and related species.

Some interesting experiments have been done recently using *Echinocereus triglochidiatus* as a stock for tricky, hardy plants such as some of the pediocacti. For stapeliads, one of the larger, stronger growing *Stapelia* species is commonly used, an alternative being *Ceropegia woodii*. For euphorbias, favourites are *E. ingens* or *E. canariensis*.

Method and tools

A good clean sharp knife is an essential tool. Cut off the top of the stock and bevel the edges so that the surface does not become concave when dry. Cut off the bottom of the scion and press together the two cut surfaces. It is important that the vascular bundles of the stock and scion are adjacent as they must unite for the flow of water and nutrients to pass from the stock to the scion.

Maintain the pressure for a few weeks while the tissues unite. The most commonly used method is to put two rubber bands round the pot and over the top of the graft, at right angles to each other. Other ideas using weights and clips have been suggested. Experiment to find what is convenient and practical for you. Once the graft has taken, put the plant in a warm place, out of direct sunshine and preferably not too dry an atmosphere. It usually takes a couple of weeks for the union to be sufficiently secure for you to release the pressure.

For some plants, variants on this flat-grafting technique, such as cutting a V-shaped wedge, can be used. Some possible arrangements are illustrated in the diagram.

Left: The diagram illustrates the variety of ways grafting can be achieved and the numerous means of attaching the stock to the scion

Pests and Diseases

Pests

Cacti and succulents, like most plants grown under intensive conditions, can be attacked by a range of pests. Their fairly tough tissue lessens the risk a little, but regular inspection is necessary to avoid problems. Many chemicals are no longer available to amateur gardeners. Always check the label for appropriate treatment and follow the manufacturer's instructions for timing and frequency.

Mealy Bug

The worst and most persistent problem is the woolly aphid or mealy bug. These look like small wood-lice, with a white woolly coating, which is waxy and protects the pest. While most other pests may damage plants, mealy bugs are capable of killing large specimens rapidly. They breed at a great rate, soon forming large colonies and also quickly acquiring resistance to pesticides. They seem to be able to lay dormant on inert material for considerable periods and to break out when conditions are favourable. The waxy and woolly covering makes it difficult for contact insecticides to penetrate. In addition, there are many species, all of which have slightly different characteristics and habits, which further compound the problem.

Root attacks One particular species of mealy bug attacks the roots of cacti. This form is seen as white patches on the roots when repotting a plant. If a plant is unaccountably sick and not growing, take it out of its pot and examine the roots. If the bugs are found, wash off all the soil and bugs in a jet of water, allow to dry and repot in fresh clean soil.

Control

Systemic insecticide The normal method is to use a systemic insecticide, usually one based on an organophosphorus compound. These can be quite effective, but many strains of mealy bug have built up some resistance to them, and it may be necessary to try more than one type. However, this has been made more difficult by the fact that some of the most effective formulations are no longer available, because it is not economic to undertake the extensive testing now required for market approval.

Washing away It is possible to wash away the bugs from some plants in a jet of water, perhaps with some wetting agent. With small infections it may be possible to squash or otherwise physically remove the bugs, which look like small woolly lumps. Some growers use methylated spirits or other forms of alcohol to dab on the insects which removes their waxing coatings and definitely kills them; however, there are dangers in damaging the plants themselves by using the alcohol.

Biological controls Biological controls are preferred to insecticides. They are often used successfully on the commercial scale, but are not always easy to use on small collections. Several predators for mealy bugs can be purchased from commercial sources, including lacewings and species of *Cryptolaemus*, which is a type of ladybird. Both will also help to control other aphid-related pests, such as scale, greenfly and whitefly. If you have a particularly bad attack of mealy bug, they may be worth considering.

Drawbacks of biological control include the fact that insecticides can no longer be used for any other pests, so you may need biological controls for them too. In addition, some of the pest must always be available, otherwise the predators will starve or go elsewhere. Many of the predators need somewhat higher temperatures than are often maintained in most cacti and succulent glasshouses.

Right: One of the most persistent pests of cacti and succulents is the mealy bug, also known as the woolly aphid

Prevention

It is easier to keep mealy bugs out of a collection of cacti and succulents than to tackle an infestation. It is a good idea to quarantine new plants to make sure that they are not carrying pests. If mealy bugs appear, it is vital to deal with them straight away before they have a chance to multiply. Good hygiene is important as mealy bugs love to hide under dead leaves or flowers and other places where you and your insecticide spray cannot reach.

Red Spider Mite

Red spider mite is less of a problem than mealy bug. These creatures are not spiders (do not confuse them with the much larger red sand spiders often seen on dry-stone walls and quite harmless to plants) but actually a parasitic mite, reddish-orange in colour. The mites are very small, so that unless you have particularly good eyesight the damage may be the first thing you see. This usually appears as brown scarring on the younger growth.

Below: Damage to a cactus done by the red spider mite

Susceptible plants

Only the minority of cacti and succulents are susceptible. Among the cacti, rebutias, lobivias and coryphanthas are most commonly attacked, but it will occasionally also go for melocactus, sulcorebutia, some mamillarias and some of the smaller Mexican globular cacti, such as lophophora, turbinicarpus and pelecyphora.

Some of the Mesembryanthemaceae, such as faucarias, are also prone to red spider mite attack. This may be a different species, as the mites appear black rather than red like those found on cacti. However, the damage and recommended treatment are the same.

Some species of caudiciform succulents are also prone to similar mite attack on the leaves of their annual vines. Again this is certainly not the same as the cactus pest and may be different again from those attacking the mesembryanthemums.

Prevention and Control

The pest is encouraged by hot, dry conditions and lack of adequate ventilation. A more humid atmosphere on its own is insufficient to prevent

recurrence, but when combined with the maximum ventilation the problem is quite rare. Persistent use of appropriate chemicals can kill the pests (check what is available at your local garden centre).

Be particularly vigilant for this pest if you have a nearby hedge of *Chamaecyparis leylandii*, which can harbour it over winter.

Scale Insects

This relatively uncommon sap-feeding pest is brown or grey-brown in colour. It is often seen on agaves and opuntias.

Control

Direct spraying with insecticide is not very effective because the insects have a hard, impenetrable shell-like coating. A systemic insecticide, which the pests will suck from the plants, can be more effective. Sometimes hand removal can be fairly easy and effective.

Western Flower Thrips

This is a relatively new pest to cacti and succulents. These small, fast-moving insects range in colour from lemon-yellow to dusky yellow-brown. They are often seen in the flowers, where they can cause distortion and lack of fertility but are unlikely to actually harm the plants.

Control

They are best controlled with sticky traps.

Slugs and Snails

These molluscs can be a problem, particularly on the more fleshy succulents.

Prevention and Control

Greenhouse hygiene is important. Locating the offenders is far more successful at night when they are active. In extreme cases it may be necessary to use slug bait.

Above: Scale insets on a yucca. Fortunately, this sap-eating pest is not very common

Ants

Ants do not actually damage the plants themselves but may introduce mealy bugs or other aphids. In extreme cases nest-building activity may upset roots.

Control

If necessary use a powdered insecticide.

Leaf Cutter Bees

These often solitary bees are hairy and black or metallic blue, green or purple. They have been a pest in greenhouses for many years. They excavate tunnels in pots where they lay eggs in carefully constructed leaf-lined cells. This can cause two problems: first the leaves can initiate rotting of the plant roots; second, if a large taproot gets in the way the bees may bore a hole straight though it. Leaf cutter bees are fond of hanging baskets, which provide an attractive warm dry spot for egg-laying.

Control

Repot the plants, removing the leaf-lined cells as soon as this activity is spotted.

Sciarid Fly (Mushroom Flies or Fungus Gnats)

These tiny flies, sooty-grey to black in colour, produce grubs that can cause problems.

The small, white grubs are rarely a danger to larger plants but can do serious damage to the roots of very young seedlings. The pest is associated almost exclusively with peat-based composts.

Control

Yellow sticky insecticidal strips trap the adult flies, breaking the breeding cycle.

Eelworm or Nematodes

Eelworms or nematodes are microscopic, transparent worm-like creatures. This pest seems largely confined to relatively warm areas and causes large, cyst-like growths on the roots, which may then cause stunting of the plants.

Control

Normal insecticides are not very effective. The usually recommended treatment is to put the plant in water at 50°C (122°F) for 15–20 minutes. There are effective chemical treatments only available to commercial growers.

Tortrix Moth Caterpillar

These caterpillars are an occasional problem with leafy succulents or mesembryanthemums. If some leaves appear stuck together with a cocoon, prise them open and you may find a small grub eating the leaves.

Control

Remove by hand.

Vine Weevil

Vine weevils are slow-moving grey-brown beetles just under 1 cm (½ in) long, with pale brown flecks on their wings. The C-shaped, cream-coloured grubs do the main damage, eating the roots and causing plants to collapse. Echeverias are the most susceptible, and occasionally aeoniums.

Control

If the stem is hollow with grubs inside, cut back the stem to a sound area, and then treat the plant as a cutting and plant in clean fresh soil, and incinerate the infected plant material. Water nematode predators, *Heterorhabiditis* spp., into warm compost.

Greenfly

Greenfly are not usually a problem on cacti and succulents, although they sometimes affect the flower spikes of aloes and haworthias.

Control

The usual chemical sprays are effective or simply remove and destroy the flower spikes.

Whitefly

Whitefly leaves most cacti and succulents alone, but leafy caudiciform succulents or succulent pelargoniums may be infested.

Control

Yellow sticky insecticidal strips help control whitefly. The problem will eventually correct itself during the dormant period.

Diseases

Cacti and succulents are susceptible to two groups of diseases – fungal and bacterial rots – and those diseases caused by mineral deficiencies in the soil.

Rotting

The main diseases of cacti and succulents are fungal and bacterial rots. Most healthy plants are able to resist these infections.

Causes

Rots commonly occur as a secondary effect of other problems, such as attack by insects, pests, physical damage leaving exposed plant tissue or incorrect growing conditions. The single biggest cause probably occurs when fungal rots enter via dead roots, which result from poor root aeration.

Prevention and Control

The best way to avoid these problems is to provide conditions that prevent their development – i.e., a healthy and pest-free environment. Look for discoloured vascular tissue, which may be red or brown, and which may penetrate some way into otherwise healthy tissue.

Cut away diseased tissue If the rots occur and are spotted early, it may be possible to save the plant by cutting away all the diseased tissue with a clean knife. Clean the knife with alcohol to prevent spreading fungal spores. It may be beneficial to dust the cut surfaces with a fungicidal powder.

Fungicidal chemicals These can give some protection, but only use them as a last result, since they are not effective against the whole range of different rot-producing fungi.

Copper fungicides Young cactus and succulent seedlings are particularly prone to damping-off, which is a fungal disease. This can be partially controlled by copper fungicides. The other frequently mentioned chemical for this purpose, chinosol, is suspected of causing some damage to seedlings and is not recommended.

Deficiency Diseases

The other group of diseases that affect succulent plants are caused by deficiencies of various minerals in the soil.

Causes

The deficiency may not be simply that the soil does not contain the required elements. The minerals may not be available as a result of watering: the soil may have become too alkaline because of the build-up of salts from minerals contained in the water used.

Prevention

Find out the alkalinity of your local water and if necessary take steps to correct it by adding suitable acid. Unless you are a chemist and have the necessary knowledge, it is inadvisable to use strong mineral acids for this purpose. It is possible to use citric acid or acetic acid (vinegar), but a popular remedy is potassium dihydrogen phosphate, which also supplies useful elements. If your local rainwater is sufficiently clean this is the best way to avoid the soil becoming alkaline.

Control

Deficiency diseases are more likely to show up in peat- rather than soil-based composts. If a plant looks chlorotic or refuses to grow properly, try fresh compost to see if this solves the problem. It may help to add appropriate supplements, if locally available soils are known to have particular deficiency problems.

Building a Collection

Creating a Collection

Creating your own collection of cacti and succulents, whether through purchases, by growing your own from seed, or both, will give great satisfaction. In your own home you can appreciate the diversity and unique features of these exotic plants.

Garden Centres and Florists

For most people, it is likely that your first plants will have been acquired from a garden centre or florist. Many of these outlets have a good selection of plants for sale from time to time.

Regrettably, however, such establishments often know little about the care of cacti and succulents. Usually when the plants arrive from the wholesaler they are in good condition. Subsequently, the plants are all too often displayed in the darkest part of the greenhouse or shop and are then incorrectly watered (either too much or too little). One result may be infestation with pests, particularly mealy bug. It is also not unknown for dead plants to be left on display.

If you are a regular visitor to garden centres and florists, keep a look out for new deliveries of plants, which you can be more confident are in good condition. The plants should have a good uniform appearance with bright colours and should not show signs of etiolation. In particular, look out for the little white woolly lumps, tell-tale signs of mealy bug.

If the plants are in flower that is probably a good sign, but watch out for the trick some wholesalers play of sticking on individual, artificial or dried flowers with glue or pins, which almost certainly will have damaged the plants. Remember that most cactus and succulent flowers are short lived, so if your cactus is apparently in flower for several weeks, look closely – you may find the blooms are artificial. Various cacti and succulent societies have tried to eliminate this practice, but in reality there is not a lot that can be done unless the plants are described as 'flowering cacti', when the trader may be in breach of trade description legislation.

Specialist Nurseries

As you gain more experience you are likely to want to buy specific species, which most probably are not so commonly available. Specialist nurseries are by far the best source: they have a good range of plants that are usually available at reasonable prices. If you

Below: A densely packed display of tall-growing cacti in the author's collection

Above: A selection of young cactus seedlings, which can be found in specialist nurseries

have a nursery in your area, visit it to get good advice as well as good plants.

Don't worry if your area doesn't have a specialist nursery as most run a good mail order service. Fortunately, cacti and succulents are well suited to the mail order business: they do not wilt in transit, are often quite compact and are reasonably robust. It is advisable not to place orders in the depth of winter because the plants may be too cold in transit.

If you want to buy plants from nurseries in other countries, you may need import/export licenses and phytosanitary certificates. However these plants can usually be moved between EU countries without any difficulty.

You can locate these nurseries through advertisements in the cacti and succulent journals published by the various National Cactus Societies. Alternatively, if you have Internet access, you can locate them through the Cactus and Succulent Plant Mall.

Growing from Seed

One of the best ways to build up a collection for little outlay is to grow plants from seed. A number of specialist seed suppliers worldwide offer an enormous range. With only a few exceptions, cactus and succulent seed has long viability, and with a little practice results can be very good. The seedlings you raise yourself will be a source of particular pleasure and often seem to adapt better to the conditions you can offer.

You will find that, even though the commercial suppliers have a very good range of plants, many species are unobtainable. They may not be in cultivation, but it is more likely there is a low demand for them or they are particularly awkward to propagate. The only way to obtain such plants is through the network of collectors who grow them. You can find them through joining national and international groups. Most collectors are only too happy to spare cuttings or seeds of unusual plants to propagate them. In many ways this acts as an insurance against the loss of a plant because it is possible to reacquire a rare plant that may have been lost because you gave away cuttings to other collectors.

Occasionally, large collections of mature plants come up for sale from a collector who is unable to look after them any longer. This can be a source of valuable mature plants, and such plants do not usually sell for particularly high prices. Taking on mature specimens that have adapted to their previous owners conditions may be tricky and is best undertaken by enthusiasts with some experience.

As your plant collection grows, so will your knowledge of the range of these intriguing plants, which, for the most part, are easy to care for, and will reward you through their unusual beauty.

Plant Directory

Cacti

Aporocactus

Commonly known as the rat's-tail cactus, *Aporocactus flagelliformis* is one of those plants frequently grown by people who do not specialize in cacti. There are good reasons for this: it has been in cultivation for a long time; it tolerates a lot of neglect; and it will grow well indoors on a sunny windowsill. It also makes a good hanging-basket plant with long cylindrical trailing stems that can reach several feet in length. This plant flowers easily in spring, producing a host of pink flowers. A lot of work has been done in creating hybrids of this species that produce larger flowers of slightly different colours.

Above: This *Ariocarpus fissuratus* has been grown from seed and is about ten years old

Ariocarpus

This small genus of very slow-growing cacti comes from northern Mexico and the southern USA. Because they are slow growing and do not get very large, they have been much prized by collectors. In the past many plants have been taken from their habitat for sale in the horticultural trade. Fortunately, this is no longer the case as the plants are protected and removal of such plants is now illegal. Seed from plants in cultivation is obtainable fairly easily, and although considerable patience is required it is perfectly possible to raise them by this method. They are not particularly difficult to grow, but some care is needed with their watering, and it is preferable to grow them in clay pots. They have a growing season later in the year than some cacti, flowering usually in late summer to early autumn. When they are in growth and flowering they can take quite heavy watering.

Ariocarpus kotschoubeyanus, a small, flat plant, is slow growing but quite easy and will flower at a small size. It grows on flat, sandy plains and is reported to be sometimes covered in water for a short period in the rainy season. *A. trigonus*, which, like *A. furfuraceus*, grows on rocky scree slopes, may be the most difficult species. The miniature species *A. agavoides* and *A. scapharostris* are both very scarce in the wild as they have only been found in one very small locality. Fortunately, both are readily available as cultivated seedling grown plants. *A. agavoides* can flower when less than 2.5 cm (1 in) in diameter. These plants cannot be recommended for indoor cultivation, as very good light is essential.

Arrojadoa

This is a small genus of rather interesting Brazilian cacti, which make small clumps of shrubby stems up to 0.6–1 m (2–3 ft) tall. The characteristic of the genus is that they develop small tufts of bristles and hairs at the tips of the stems from which the small, waxy and usually pink flowers develop. They are quite easy to grow, provided they are given a minimum winter temperature that is a little higher than the average – say 10°C (50°F). They grow fairly rapidly and can be expected to flower in three to four years from seed and certainly when they are less than 30 cm (1 ft) high.

The thicker stemmed species, such as *Arrojadoa rhodantha* and *A. aureispina*, are the most robust, while the thinner stemmed species, such as *A. eriocaulis* or *A. penicillata*, may need a small amount of water in winter to prevent the stems from drying up. They are likely to be available from only a few specialist nurseries or stockists.

Astrophytum

This very distinct genus of globular cacti occurs in southern USA and northern Mexico. The astrophytums are distinguished by having a white 'speckling' on the epidermis. Because of this feature, their distinctive form and attractive yellow flowers they are very popular with collectors. Although they are not suitable for indoor cultivation, they are not difficult to grow under the right conditions. Use a well-drained, mineral-based compost for best results. A very sunny position is advised. They are quite cold tolerant and will not be harmed by near-freezing temperatures as long as they are dry.

There are only a few species, but these come in a host of variations; also, many hybrids and cultivars have been produced, so it is possible to collect quite a large number of 'different' plants. Astrophytums are usually solitary stemmed, branching only if the growing point has been damaged. The largest growing and perhaps the easiest to cultivate is *Astrophytum ornatum*. It can grow to 100 cm (3 ft) or more in height and 15–20 cm (6–8 in) in diameter, although it will take many years to reach this size. As a younger plant this is globular and can be expected to flower at around five to six years old and 8 cm (3 in) in diameter.

Perhaps the most common species is *A. myriostigma*, sometimes known as the bishop's hat cactus because of its shape. This is smaller than *A. ornatum* and lacks spines, it will also start flowering when smaller. The species is quite variable in the wild, and a number of different forms are in cultivation.

A. capricorne's main characteristic is a dense birds-nest array of flexible, twisted spines over the plant body. These are variable in colour and density, as is the spotting on the stem. The flower is probably the best of the genus, being larger and usually having a red centre in a yellow flower. Success with it is more difficult because it is somewhat prone to root loss if it is kept too wet, and it can then be difficult to re-establish.

A. asterias is another spineless astrophytum which has a form very reminiscent of a sea-urchin. This is rather slower growing than the other species and also needs care to avoid overwatering. We struggled to grow a good specimen of this species for some years; then we reverted to growing it in a porous clay pot, which has proved much more successful. This species is more likely to be found only at a specialist nursery.

Below: ***Astrophytum capricorne*** **is even more variable and slightly more difficult in cultivation than other Astrophytums**

Above: *Carnegia gigantea*, **although frequently seen as a seedling plant, is not very successful outside its native habitat because to grow well it needs high temperatures and a free root run**

Carnegiea

This genus contains only one species, *Carnegiea gigantea*. It is the giant columnar cactus that grows in mainly southern Arizona and adjacent areas of Mexico. It eventually reaches more than 12.25 m (40 ft) in height and weighs many tons. It is very slow growing, and the largest plants are probably 200–300 years old. Branching and flowering do not commence until the plants are several metres high, which may take some 40 years, even under favourable conditions.

Cephalocereus

This genus used to contain many species, but most have been transferred to other genera within recent years. The remaining species, *Cephalocereus senilis,* is commonly known as the old man cactus because of its long, flexible, whiskery spines. It is attractive as a seedling and easy to grow, if a somewhat slow grower. It is very commonly available as seedlings in garden centres. The plants come from an area in the state of Hidalgo in Mexico called the Barranca de Metitzlan. This particular large valley has a very rich cactus flora containing very many beautiful cactus species growing in natural rock gardens. Here specimens of *C. senilis* grow to impressive plants more than 6 m (20 ft) tall. They will not flower until they are large plants, at least 2.5 m (8 ft) high, so do not expect this to happen in pot culture.

Cereus

These are mostly very fast-growing and robust plants. Many rapidly get too large for the average greenhouse and in fact will not flower until they are quite large. However, a couple of species are worth looking out for because they start to flower at under 100 cm (3 ft) in height. Both come from the Brazilian–Argentinian border and grow happily in normal greenhouse conditions. *Cereus chalybaeus* has slate-blue stems and short black spines. The flowers are nocturnal, white with a pinkish tube and about 15 cm (6 in) long and 10 cm (4 in) in diameter. They have a delicate perfume. *C. azureus* is more slender, and its larger flowers are not produced in quite such profusion.

Below: Specimen of *Cereus peruvianus* f. *monstrosus*. **This is one of the unusual growth forms** **(see page 15)**

Cleistocactus

This interesting group of columnar cacti deserves to be more widely grown. They can grow very quickly under favourable conditions, and many species will flower prolifically. Because they are large, quickly growing cacti, they appreciate plenty of water and frequent doses of fertilizer. They need large pots or a free root run and only a relatively short dormant dry spell in the winter. They originate in Andean valleys in Peru and Bolivia. They are tolerant of quite low temperatures, certainly down to freezing, although probably not below this without sustaining some damage.

The most commonly seen species, *Cleistocactus strausii*, which is covered in dense white spines, is certainly eye-catching but is not so freely flowering as some other species. To flower it needs to grow to at least 45 cm/18 in high and to be in good light. The flowers are a dusky red and long and tubular in shape. Like all the species of *Cleistocactus* they are pollinated by humming-birds.

Other recommendable species include *C. flavescens* (yellow flowered), *C. brookei* (red flowered) and *C. vulpis-cauda* (also red flowered and softly spined; the name means fox's tail, and unlike most cacti it can be stroked with impunity). These will all flower at around 23 cm (9 in) tall. Also recommended are *C. dependens* and some forms of *C. baumannii*.

Copiapoa

Native to the dry coastal deserts of northern Chile, in the wild these interesting globular cacti get much of their moisture from the frequent coastal mists, many receiving little direct rainfall. They are slow growing, eventually forming large 'barrels' or clumps, which are thought to be over 100 years in age.

Surprisingly, they take quite well to cultivation, although most species remain slow growing and some will not start flowering until 10–20 years old. They prefer a mineral-based soil without a great deal of humus in it. In hot climates it is very important to give them plenty of ventilation as it is surprisingly easy to scorch them. Periodic mist spraying is beneficial. The flowers are all rather similar – yellow and between 2.5–5 cm (1–2 in) in diameter.

Above: ***Copiapoa humilis*** **is one of the faster growing of this genus, and will start flowering when it is four years old from seed**

The rather softer bodied species such as *Copiapoa humilis* are the fastest growing and will commence flowering when around four years old from seed. Some of the very stoutly spined species, such as *C. cinerea,* are quite slow and may need to be 12–15 years old before they will start flowering. With age some develop interesting body colours; for example, *C. cinerea* becomes chalky white.

Coryphantha

This group of mostly fairly small globular cacti comes from northern Mexico and southern USA. They are not particularly difficult to grow, although for best results they do prefer good sunny light conditions, so they are probably not suitable for indoor cultivation. Most species have strong spines and are quite attractive, even when not in flower. The majority have yellow flowers, which are borne at the crown of the plant around midsummer; a few have pink flowers. While some species remain solitary and will not grow more than 5–8 cm (2–3 in) in diameter, others offset produce and form clumps with large numbers of heads. A characteristic of the genus is that the spine clusters and areoles are borne at the tips of tubercles, which are separated and do not form ribs. The flowers come from a groove in the top of the tubercle, which is connected to the areole.

One of the most common and easiest to grow species is *Coryphantha bumamma*. This has broad, glossy, dark green tubercles and clear, yellow flowers about 5 cm (2 in) in diameter. It can form quite large clumps with age. Much smaller are plants like *C. radians*, which has a dense covering of yellow radial spines and rarely offsets. The flowers are yellow.

Some species, such as *C. erecta,* form clusters of more elongated stems; this is more reluctant to flower in cultivation, requiring very sunny conditions. There are a few rarer species, such as *C. macromeris* and *C. scheeri,* which are a little more difficult in cultivation. They require more careful watering and perhaps little humus in the soil.

Echinocactus

Native to Mexico and the southern USA, this is a small group of barrel cacti. The best known plant in cultivation is *Echinocactus grusonii*, often called the golden barrel or, more unkindly, mother-in-law's chair. It is a beautiful plant and one that has adapted well to cultivation. This is just as well because it is relatively rare in the wild, being somewhat localized in an area of Mexico where there is now a hydro-electric power scheme. This plant is grown in huge numbers by the wholesale cactus nurseries and is frequently seen in garden centres. Larger plants are grown outdoors in the southern USA and for the European market in such places as

Above: ***Echinocactus grusonii*, a barrel cactus, which is often called the golden barrel**

Tenerife and Israel. This is one of those plants that will tolerate a lot of abuse in cultivation and still survive. Under ideal conditions it grows quite quickly and can eventually reach several feet in diameter and height. Flowers, rather small and insignificant, are produced only on fairly old plants, under good conditions.

When it is kept dry, *E. grusonii* may survive mild frosts, but in most European countries, where winters are wet, it should be kept above freezing or the epidermis may be marked.

Less common in cultivation but more widespread in the wild is *E. ingens*. This species is less tolerant of maltreatment but forms magnificent large barrels in the wild and can also be grown well in cultivation. In a pot it remains slow and seems to respond best to free root run conditions in an open bed.

The range of *E. horizonthalonius* spreads up into the Big Bend National Park area of Texas, as well as growing in Mexico. It is a much smaller growing species but is not a plant for the beginner. It needs a light touch: careful watering, little humus in the compost and a sunny, light position in the greenhouse. Grow this species in a clay rather than a plastic pot so that it dries out quickly after watering. It is well worth the effort as the body is a greyish-blue and the very pretty pink flowers appear on quite small plants.

E. texensis (formerly *Homalocephala texensis*) is a plant of a similar nature to the previous species but is easier to cultivate. It is known locally as the horse crippler because of its very sharp, strong spines. There are also some species of *Echinocactus* that occur in the Mojave Desert in southern California and the Grand Canyon. These plants form magnificent multi-headed clumps in these very arid areas and are among the most difficult cacti to cultivate. They are rarely seen in cultivation and should be attempted only by experts with ideal conditions.

Echinocereus

This group of low-growing, clumping cacti have beautiful, long-lasting flowers, making them very popular with collectors. They come from northern Mexico and the USA, some growing at surprisingly northerly latitudes and quite high altitudes. Because of this quite a few species are hardy and can be grown outside under the right conditions. The common American name for these plants is the hedgehog cactus. They can be recognized by their very spiny flower tube.

Some species of *Echinocereus* can be reluctant to produce their flowers. The usual reason for this is that it is important that they have their cool (or even cold) dry winter rest period. Keeping them too warm in winter may inhibit flowering. For some species of *Echinocereus* it is also important to have good light conditions so they are best grown in a greenhouse, conservatory or frame.

Above: *Echinocereus* var. *rubrispinus* is a recent discovery with an attractive form and pink flowers

Echinocereus are unusual in that the flower bud develops within the body of the cactus and then bursts through the stem. This can leave a small scar, and, even under favourable conditions, the dead flowers can cause stem rot. It is important therefore to remove the dead flowers, particularly in damp weather.

Many species are worth growing, and also most of the species have a fair number of local forms, so it is possible to have quite a large collection of this genus. Some of the less spiny Mexican species are among the easiest to grow and flower. *Echinocereus knippelianus* grows into small clumps of globular heads and has attractive pink flowers in spring. *E. pulchellus* is similar, but has more ribs and is spinier. *E. sheerii* is a larger growing species, which forms clumps of more elongated stems. This species and a number of closely related ones, such as *E. salm-dykianus* and *E. gentryi*, have long-tubed flowers, which tend to stay open into the evening. They are very easy to grow and flower. Growing at high altitudes in Mexico is the hairy *E. delaetii*. This is much more reluctant to flower in cultivation unless very good light can be provided.

Some species of *Echinocereus*, such as *E. enneacanthus*, form very large clumps of heads. They can also be somewhat more reluctant to flower if given too much water, heat and/or nitrogenous food when they will grow rampantly. The large and long-lasting flowers are worth waiting for. *E. pentalophus* is similar with rather straggly unattractive stems but beautiful flowers. Much neater is *E. pectinatus*, sometimes called the rainbow cactus because of its attractive coloured spines. These plants occur on both sides of the Mexican–USA border and come in a wide range of forms. A particularly attractive form was discovered about 20 years ago and is usually called *E.* var. *rubrispinus*. The flower is pink and some 10 cm (4 in) in diameter.

Also very attractive and relatively small growing is *E. reichenbachii*, some forms of which grow as far north as Oklahoma and will take quite cold conditions if dry in winter. The same is true of *E. chloranthus*, which has forms with small greenish or brownish flowers.

E. engelmannii, which has needle-like spines, can also form quite large clumps of attractive stems. It will withstand quite cold conditions but is not tolerant of damp. The large flowers are unusually beautiful but will form only if the light conditions are good and if the plant is not too warm in winter. *E. triglochidiatus* is a common US species and occurs in a wide variety of forms. Some grow at surprisingly high altitudes and far north in the USA and are quite hardy. They sometimes form big clumps and can be quite spectacular when they are in flower in spring. The rich orange-red flowers are quite large; unlike many cactus flowers, they do not close up at night. The common name is the claret-cup cactus.

Echinopsis

Plants of the genus *Echinopsis* are very common in cultivation for several good reasons: they are mostly very easy to grow, they take well to indoor cultivation, and they will tolerate a lot of bad cultivation and neglect. They are also common because they offset freely and the offsets root very easily. So, given even moderately good conditions they will flower and, as the flowers are mostly large and sometimes nicely scented, they are much appreciated but rather short lived. Because they have been in cultivation for some time, quite a lot of hybridizing has been done, intentionally and unintentionally, and a good range of attractive flower coloured forms is available.

Above: A beautiful large flower typical of the genus *Echinopsis*

It is slightly unfortunate that taxonomists pointed out in the early 1990s that it is not possible to draw a clear dividing line between the plants in *Echinopsis* and those in the genus *Trichocereus*. The latter have more or less identical flowers, but on the whole grow much larger and taller and are therefore not quite so well suited to cultivation. Plants of *Trichocereus* may sometimes be encountered under the generic name *Echinopsis* but cannot be expected to flower until they are considerably larger than plants in *Echinopsis*.

Species, such as *Echinopsis eyriesii*, *E. tubiflora*, *E. multiplex* and *E. oxygona*, which have been cultivated for a long time, are probably rare as pure species, but many plants derived from them are widely available and are well worth growing. The flowers are mostly white or pink and can be as large as 20 cm (8 in) long and 15 cm (6 in) in diameter. It is a myth that they will flower better if the offsets are removed. Given a good amount of root room, they will develop into large clumps and bear many flowers. The yellow-flowered *E. aurea* is slightly less common but also makes a good clump; it is often one parent of some of the yellow-flowered hybrids.

Some of the slightly smaller echinopsis were formerly included in the genus *Pseudolobivia*. They usually have smaller flowers but make up for it by producing large numbers. If these plants are kept in a hot greenhouse, put them in a shaded position as they can lose large quantities of water when they produce a big crop of flowers. Typical species of this group are *E. ancistrophora* and *E. polyancistra*. Two species with very striking coloured flowers are *E. kermesina* (carmine-red) and *E. frankii* (deep pink).

Epiphyllum

These are commonly known as the orchid cacti. The species of the genus are relatively scarce in cultivation and do not do particularly well in a normal cactus greenhouse. In the wild they mostly grow epiphytically alongside orchids and bromeliads and need similar conditions. However, there has been more intentional hybridizing in this group than within any other group of cacti. This has not only produced a very large number of plants with spectacular flowers, but has also introduced greater hybrid vigour and tolerance of a wider range of conditions. Thus many of the hybrids make good indoor plants as long as they are grown in reasonable light.

Below: **A delicately hued hybrid *Epiphyllum***

Above: **The stunning flower of a large hybrid *Epiphyllum***

The epiphyllums need different conditions from the very xerophytic globular cacti. They require a richer soil with more humus in it and a fertilizer with a rather higher percentage of nitrogen. While the hybrids are more resistant to cold than the species, they still appreciate rather more winter warmth than most cacti. The hybrid epiphyllums may have flowers up to 25 cm (10 in) in diameter and almost all flower colours (except blue) have been developed. Some forms with *E. cooperi* in their parentage also have a strong perfume.

Surprisingly, epiphyllums are not often seen in garden centres, perhaps because their flowering season is rather short and the plants are not particularly attractive when not in flower. To find a good range of species go to a nursery that specializes in epiphyllums of which there are one or two in most large countries.

Espostoa

These plants originate in the Peruvian Andes and make very attractive specimens. Most species are covered with a dense white wool and, although eventually they get quite large, they are not fast growing so are quite popular in cultivation. In the wild they grow in very rocky soil on the sides of fairly steep valleys, but they are quite accommodating and seem to grow well in any well-drained soil. They are fairly tolerant of cold conditions but should be kept frost free for safety.

Like many plants of the Andes, each valley has its own population, which differs slightly from those in adjacent valleys and has been given a different species name although the differences are marginal. *Espostoa lanata* is the oldest name for the larger growing species, which will eventually reach 2.5–2.75 m (8–9 ft) in height with fairly strong spines as well as the wool. *E. melanostele* rarely exceeds 1 m (3 ft) in height and has more fluffy, dense, white wool, and most forms are not so strongly spined.

When espostoas reach flowering size they produce a modified area in a groove on the side of the stem at the top. The areoles in this area produce copious wool and bristles and will eventually flower; this structure is called a cephalium. The plants need to be a fair age to get to this stage and conditions must be ideal, so flowering plants are not often seen in cultivation. It is believed that one of the factors delaying the production of the cephalium in cultivation is the unequal summer/winter daylight length in more northerly latitudes.

The plants formerly included in the genus *Thrixanthocereus* are now generally included in *Espostoa*. They come from slightly further north in Peru and are not quite so tolerant of cold temperatures but are otherwise fairly easy to grow. They form their bristly cephaliums at slightly smaller sizes than espostoas do. *E. senilis* has pure white spines, while *E. blossfeldiorum* has grey and black ones.

Below: ***Espostoa melanostele*** **exhibiting the dense white wool that, in its natural habitat, protects it from extremes of temperature**

Ferocactus

This group of attractive spiny barrel cacti is from Mexico and the USA. Some grow to quite large sizes and do not flower very easily in cultivation. However, they do make imposing specimens and are therefore quite popular. They are also easy to grow from seed, which is produced in large quantities, resulting in their being seen frequently in garden centres.

Most species do best in a compost without too much humus and benefit from being given a fairly large root run so that they can grow to maturity. One particular problem that can occur with some species arises from the fact that they have a gland on the areole that secretes a sugary substance. In damp conditions this

Above: ***Ferocactus chrysacanthus*****, one of the smaller species, has a dense covering of fierce golden spines**

encourages the growth of the mould *Aspergillus niger*, which does not damage the plant but can be very unsightly. It can be brushed away with a small brush but this is time consuming and fiddly. Spraying with water at the right time to remove the nectar can work. In some greenhouses the nectar is collected by ants, which certainly minimizes the problem. In drier climates this is unlikely to be a problem.

There are a few species that do not normally grow quite so large, and these would be best for the beginner. *Ferocactus* (*Hamatocactus*) *setispinus* is a small, very free-flowering species that will do well on a windowsill or in the greenhouse. The flowers are yellow with a red centre, and the plant carries on flowering throughout the summer. The remaining species are probably better suited to greenhouse than indoor cultivation. *F. macrodiscus* is also small. It forms a broad, flat head rarely more than 15 cm (6 in) in diameter. It will produce attractive striped flowers at half this size. Slightly larger is *F. latispinus*, which will grow up to 30 cm (12 in) across and has characteristic broad, flattened spines. This species needs very good light to fully develop its characteristics. There are forms with red spines and purple flowers and with yellow spines and yellow flowers. Of similar size is *F. viridescens*, which grows near the coast in southern California and the adjacent Baja California peninsula. The name refers to the yellowish-green flowers.

F. glaucescens can be found growing alongside *Cephalocereus senilis* and *Astrophytum ornatum* in the Barranca de Metitzlan of eastern Mexico. As the name suggests, it has a slightly glaucous stem, which can grow to around 30 cm (12 in) in diameter. This species will offset to form small clumps of up to six to eight heads. The spines are yellow, as are the flowers. It needs to be around ten years old before it will flower. *F. robustus* has quite small heads, growing to only 15 cm (6 in) or so in diameter but developing into large clumps of several hundred heads. This species appears to be somewhat reluctant to flower in cultivation.

F. stainesii is one of the larger growing and most striking species of *Ferocactus*. In the wild huge red-spined specimens with main stems 2.5 m (8 ft) tall and 60 cm (2 ft) in diameter and a dozen or so slightly smaller offsets can be found. It has attractive rings of orange-red flowers on the crown. In cultivation it seems to be fairly slow growing, and our largest plant has not reached flowering size although it must be a fair age.

Also large, although it usually remains solitary, is *F. wislizenii*, which grows in the same habitat as *Carnegia* and needs the same sunny, hot conditions. It has strong hooked spines and yellow flowers. Also from Arizona but spreading into California is *F. acanthodes* with long twisting red spines. This species tends to be slow growing in areas where it does not get the sun and heat it prefers.

Gymnocalycium

The gymnocalyciums originate in South America, where they cover quite a wide area, including Argentina, Paraguay, Uruguay and parts of Bolivia. They are easy to grow and flower, since they are tolerant of a wide range of conditions. The genus can be recognized by the scaly flower buds.

Gymnocalycium bruchii comes in a wide variety of forms but is characterized by fairly small heads, which proliferate into quite large clumps. It bears pale pink to whitish flowers. *G. baldianum* is very common and popular. It also flowers very easily with red to purplish flowers and it does offset, but not quite as freely as *G. bruchii*. *G. andreae* is similar with a clear yellow flower. *G. quehlianum* is a little slower growing and tends to remain solitary. This species has silver-white flowers. There are also some quite large-growing species in the genus, such as *G. saglionis*. This can make quite impressive specimens up to 45 cm (18 in) in diameter. The disadvantage is that it needs to be a little larger, around 10 cm (4 in), before it starts flowering. In spite of its name, *G. multiflorum* is not as free flowering as some species, but the flowers are larger than average for the genus.

Below: The large white flowers of *Gymnocalycium denudatum*

Above: *Gymnocalycium mihanovichii* will flower when quite small but is fairly difficult to grow

G. mihanovichii is more difficult to grow than some, preferring slightly warmer conditions, but it will flower when quite small. There is a wide range of forms, some of which have attractive purplish bodies. It has also given rise to one of the oddities of the cactus world. When cacti are grown from seed, mutant seedlings occur that lack chlorophyll. Normally these would perish, being unable to photosynthesize and manufacture food. However, in Japan some seedlings were grafted onto a green stock plant. Because they still contain the red pigment, which shows as purple in the normal plant, these seedlings are bright red. They have been extensively propagated and are sometimes sold under the name Hibotan. They must always be grown grafted and it is best to regraft periodically to retain the vigour. Further variants of this plant with pink pigment or yellow plants without the red pigment are also available.

Also worth a place in any collection is *G. horridispinum*. Strongly spined, it grows slightly taller and forms occasional offsets. It produces clear pink flowers. *G. gibbosum* is a widespread species with stout spines and large white flowers. Some forms come from southern Argentina, making them cold tolerant. *G. denudatum* has stems with a rather small number of ribs and offsets to form small clumps; the large flowers are white. *G. horstii* is quick growing and can make quite large clumps. The flowers range from pinkish to salmon in colour.

Lobivia

The genus name is an anagram of Bolivia, their country of origin, although some of the species are found in adjacent areas of Peru. All grow at high altitudes. They adapt well to cultivation and are free flowering, the flowers being rather short lived but diurnal as opposed to the related nocturnal-flowering echinopsis. They need good light and prefer not to be too warm in winter, which can inhibit flowering.

Lobivia silvestrii (syn. *Chamaecereus silvestrii*) can put on massive displays of orange flowers and is exceedingly easy to propagate from cuttings. It needs plenty of food and water in the growing season, but must have a cool, dry resting period to flower well. It is one of those cacti that hybridizes freely. There are many hybrids with a wide range of flower colours. It also hybridizes with plants from other cactus genera.

Below: ***Lobivia jajoiana*** **has many different flower colours. It rarely offsets and remains small**

Many lobivias, such as *L. densispina*, are extremely variable, particular in flower and spine colour, and a large number of different forms can be collected. The constant characteristic is that of dense spination.

Lobivias are affected by their growing conditions – for example, those grown in poor light will have elongated stems and poor spines compared to a plant grown in good light. *L. jajoiana* is also variable in having many flower colours. It tends to remain smaller than *L. densipina* and rarely offsets. It is easily recognized when in flower as the base of the stamens are fused to form a dark collar at the base of the flower. *L. backebergii* has rather ordinary green stems but offsets into big clumps and is easy to grow and flower; the flowers are red. *L. winteriana* tends to remain smaller, has few offsets and delicate pink flowers. *L. shieliana* has small shoots, which multiply to form clumps of many heads; the spines are curly and in some forms white or cream, and the flowers are brick red. With even smaller heads is *L. arachnacantha* with either red or yellow flowers. Its appearance is like that of a miniature echinopsis.

This distinct group grow into giant plants, which are sometimes put into a separate genus, *Soehrensia*. They have close affinities with some species of *Trichocereus*. They can grow to several feet in diameter and height but will not flower until considerably larger than the other lobivias. Typical is *L. bruchii*. A species with fine long spines is *L. formosa*. These plants need large pots or even a free root run to attain their full potential.

Haageocereus

Haageocereus is a genus of columnar cacti originating in Peru. Many species have dense golden-yellow spines. They are easy to raise from seed and are often propagated by cactus nurseries. They need good sunny conditions to develop properly, so they are not very suitable for indoor cultivation. Flowering is rare except in good conditions or where plants are given a free root run. There are many slightly different forms with a range of different names, of which *Haageocereus versicolor* is perhaps the most often seen. *H. decumbens* is different in that it has procumbent rather than erect stems; it is easier to flower than the erect forms.

Hildewinteria

There is only one species in this genus, *Hildewinteria aureispina*. This plant has golden-yellow spines and grows stems to 0.6–1 m (2–3 ft) long and offsets freely to form fair-sized clumps. Because of its rather spreading, trailing habit, it can be a little difficult to accommodate. The best way to display it is in a normal pot placed on a pedestal above the level of the other plants. It is extremely good for flowers and probably has the longest flowering season of almost any cactus.

Lophophora

This genus includes only a few species, but they are well known, if not notorious. The plant known as *Lophophora williamsii* is also known as the peyote cactus or dumpling cactus, and it contains a series of hallucinogenic alkaloids. The Native Americans knew this and used it in their religious ceremonies. The effects of these alkaloids have been studied in detail both by scientists and amateur experimenters, who describe vivid, multicoloured hallucinations. Unfortunately for the experimenters, the cacti also contain alkaloids that have a strong emetic effect, so the side-effects of eating the cactus are frequently unpleasant. Limited information suggests that in cultivation, at least in Europe, plants do not produce as high concentrations of the alkaloids as they do in the wild. In the USA and a few other countries growing and possessing these plants is illegal. In Europe the plant is widely grown and does not cause any difficulties, but if you are in any doubt, check your local regulations.

L. williamsii is an easy plant to grow and flower. It grows over a wide area of northern Mexico and is also found in southern Texas. There is quite a range of different forms, all spineless. The larger headed forms are slower to form clumps; they often have slightly bluish bodies and tufted yellow wool in the areoles. The more rapidly proliferating forms seem more reluctant to flower. The flower colour ranges from very pale pink to deep purplish-pink.

Mammillaria

The genus *Mammillaria* is one of the largest genera of cacti and certainly one of the most popular. There are probably around 300 species, occurring mostly in Mexico and the

Below: ***Mammillaria hahniana*** **is a slow-growing, clump-forming plant with long white hair**

USA but with a few species from the West Indies and the northern coast of South America. Because of its popularity two specialist societies are well established, publishing quarterly journals in English and German.

Many mammillarias make ideal plants for beginners as they grow quickly and easily from seed and will flower when they are quite young. Although they often have only small flowers, they frequently make up for it by producing them in large numbers. Many species offset freely and can produce quite large, spectacular clumps. Mammillarias are tolerant of a wide range of soils except for just a few difficult species that are slower growing and may need a slightly more gritty mix.

Perhaps the most commonly seen species is *Mammillaria zeilmanniana* with rings of deep pink flowers and short hooked spines. It offsets to produce quite big clumps. Although easy as small plants, larger clumps can be a bit more temperamental, and slightly more careful watering is advised. There is a white-flowered form as well, but this lacks some of the character of its more widely grown cousin.

M. bocasana is similar but is covered in white wool and has white to slightly pinkish flowers. It can develop into sizeable clumps in cultivation. *M. bombycina* can grow even larger, eventually reaching several feet in diameter with many hundreds of heads. The spines are longer, and there are different forms with both yellow and brown spines. The flowers are pinkish. *M. camptotricha* can also grow into quite large clumps with long tubercles and long twisted spines. The flowers are small and white and have a distinct perfume.

Some species of *Mammillaria* are very variable. The constant feature of *M. elongata* is the elongated stem, but there are dozens of forms, with different spine colours and arrangements and different stem sizes. All can make fair-sized clumps and have small white to cream flowers. Smaller again, but very common, is *M. gracilis*, whose shoots are weakly attached and readily fall off and root. Flowers and central spines are not produced until the central head is a reasonable size.

Above: *Mammillaria elegans*

M. geminispina also makes a large, splendid specimen with strong white spines and is very easy to grow but rather more reluctant to flower until it is quite large. Some mammillarias have quite large, showy flowers. Although *M. longimamma* is perhaps not as attractive as some species, it produces yellow flowers up to 5 cm (2 in) in diameter. The flowers of *M. surculosa* are a little smaller, but they also have a citrus smell. It makes a mass of small heads, which spread across the soil, and large clumps can produce many flowers.

M. candida is an attractive white-spined plant that occasionally offsets. It likes a good sunny position. *M. elegans* can be quite slow growing and has tiny red flowers. At the other end of the scale, *M. guelzowiana*, although superficially like *M. bocasana*, has very large flowers of an intense pinkish-red. It is distinctly more difficult and should be in a well-drained compost and watered with care.

M. matudae is very free flowering and can make a good plant, although the heads sometimes become rather long and pendant, making the plant difficult to accommodate. Various forms of *M. woodsii* are frequently seen. This can make quite large single heads, although it will occasionally offset. The amount of wool is variable, but the flowers are always small and pink. *M. plumosa* is a popular species because of its feathery spines. It has an unusual habit of flowering in winter but does not do so in cultivation unless a reasonable amount of winter sunshine is available.

Various forms of *M. rhodantha* are common in cultivation. Like *M. elongata*, this species comes in a wide range of spine colours. As with a few other mammillarias, it sometimes undergoes a splitting of the growing point into two or more growing points. This is termed dichotomous branching. Another plant that does this is *M. parkinsonii*; it has dense white spines. *M. spinosissima* is yet another excellent flowering plant, frequently having several rings of flowers open together. Of a rather different type is *M. heyderi*, which forms usually solitary broad flat heads.

There are many species of choice, dwarf mammillaria to delight the specialist collector, such as *M. herrerae* with dense interlacing white spines on a body often not much more than 2.5 cm (1 in) in diameter and quite large pink flowers. Most mammillarias are worth growing, and a good collection will provide interest and flowers for much of the year.

Below: *Mammillaria deherdtiana* is another recently discovered miniature

Above: *Mammillaria nazacensis* is a recently discovered miniature species, which benefits from a fairly gritty compost

Matucana

These are Peruvian plants, many growing at high altitudes, thus needing very good light. They have attractive spines and are well worth growing. Some species will offset, forming small clumps. *Matucana haynei* is perhaps the most common species in cultivation. It is quite variable, having forms with slightly different spine and flower colours, which range from carmine to scarlet. The flowers are about 5 cm (2 in) long and zygomorphic in shape. *M. aureiflora* has large, somewhat flattened heads, is less spiny and is atypical in having regular yellow flowers. A group of less spiny matucanas, including *M. paucicostata* and *M. madisoniorum*, grow at lower altitudes.

Melocactus

These plants are found in a number of countries. All need higher than average minimum winter temperatures to survive, as they come from relatively warm areas.

A number of species come from the West Indies. Some are found in southern Mexico, and also the north coast of South America. A further group is found in the coastal valleys of Peru. There are also a considerable number of Brazilian species. The characteristic of the genus is the terminal cephalium from which the flowers and fruits are produced.

All the species are globular or short and cylindrical. When the plants become mature, the areoles at the apex of the plants modify, forming a large amount of wool and frequently reddish bristles. No new photosynthetic plant tissue is produced, but the cephalium can continue to grow for many years. The small, pink flowers pop out of the cephalium in the afternoon. The pink fruits follow some months later. Most species appear to be self-fertile, and large quantities of flowers, fruits and seed are produced by mature plants. The size of the plants varies quite considerably from species to species, and the larger growing species naturally take longer to reach maturity. Younger plants seem more resistant to lower temperatures than mature plants with cephalia.

Probably the easiest species are the Brazilian ones. Plants such as *Melocactus concinnus* and *M. bahiensis* can be grown from seed to flowering size in eight to ten years. Melocacti tend to have wide-spreading roots and appreciate being grown in pans. They are also not very tolerant of alkaline soil, so it is important not to allow alkaline deposits to build up in the soil. Do not give melocacti too long a winter rest; some water in winter is definitely beneficial. *M. azureus*, a Brazilian species with a beautiful blue body, seems to be a little more difficult than *M. bahiensis* and must be kept reasonably warm.

The melocacti from the coastal areas of Venezuela and Mexico and the West Indian islands are mostly larger growing than the Brazilian species, making very handsome spiny specimens if kept sufficiently warm. The one exception is *M. matanzanus* from Cuba, which is perhaps the smallest melocactus, forming a cephalium when around six years old and 8 cm (3 in) in diameter. The cephalium has dense red bristles, making it very striking.

The melocacti from Peru are perhaps the least cultivated and most difficult of the genus. They grow in very arid areas and are sensitive to excess moisture. Some, such as *M. belavistensis*, are very attractive plants.

All of the melocacti appreciate as much sun as possible.

Neobuxbaumia

This small group of Mexican cerei was formerly included in *Cephalocereus*, but these plants do not produce a cephalium before flowering. They get quite large and need plenty of room. All are night flowering, and once they reach flowering size, possible in cultivation, they produce quite large numbers of flowers.

The quickest- and easiest- growing species is *Neobuxbaumia euphorbioides* from northern Mexico. It can grow 15–20 cm (6–8 in) a year and starts flowering at 1.2–1.5 m (4–5 ft). The flowers are pale pink and 5 cm (2 in) across. It grows better if kept at more than 5°C (41°F).

N. polylopha comes from central Mexico and is slower growing, at least in its younger stages. The stem is a good deal thicker and has many more ribs and grows at a rate of 5–8 cm (2–3 in) a year. Our plant that is around 1.2 m (4 ft) tall started flowering in 1996. The flowers are smaller than *N. euphorbioides* and a deeper red. We find this species marks fairly easily unless kept warmer. It is therefore quite surprising that large specimens of this species are grown outside in the exotic gardens in Monaco and other places on the French Riviera. It can eventually grow to more than 6 m (20 ft). Other species such as *N. tetetzo* appear not to take well to cultivation.

Neoporteria

This is a group of mostly small plants coming from Chile with a few species from Argentina and Peru. They take well to greenhouse cultivation and will flower at small sizes. They do need good light and are probably unlikely to flower in indoor cultivation. Many come from quite arid areas and need a well-drained mineral compost and careful watering, particularly those species that have large taproots. The taxonomists have been busy in this group, so you may also find the plants under the generic names of *Neochilenia*, *Pyrrhocactus* and *Horridocactus*.

The plants of the *Neochilenia* group are the smallest and mostly have large taproots. They can be very free flowering, even as quite young plants. The flowers are usually rather subtle colours – pale pinks and creams are common – and about 5 cm (2 in) in diameter. Often the body colours are also interesting, with shades of purple and brown pigments. They slowly offset to form small clumps. Typical species are *Neoporteria napina* and *N. esmeraldana*. There are some slightly larger, more spiny species in this group, such as *N. paucicostata*.

Below: ***Neoporteria villosa*** **displays its small pink flowers and bird's nest appearance**

Plants belonging to the genus *Neoporteria* in the narrower sense usually have very dense, bird's nest-like spines. Their smallish pink flowers have a characteristic, partially opened appearance and paler centres. On some species the flowers unusually appear in autumn to winter. Their spines make them very attractive plants. With age they become quite a bit taller than they are wide. Typical are *N. villosa*, *N. wagenknecktii and N. nidus*.

A further group of stoutly spined plants has been placed in *Horridocactus*. They have unusual coppery- or greenish-coloured flowers. On the whole they need to be slightly larger to flower than the other species. Typical of this group is *N. tubersiculata*.

Notocactus

This popular group of cacti occurs in Uruguay, Paraguay, Argentina and southern Brazil. For the most part easy to grow and flower, they make good indoor plants. They prefer an acid, peat-based compost and should not be given too long a dry rest period. Many species are worth growing, and quite a wide range of forms and flower colours is available.

Notocactus ottonis is a very common species which occurs over quite a wide area; in consequence there are a number of different forms. It forms underground stolons and eventually produces clumps of quite a few heads. The flowers are a clear yellow, appear in the spring and are 5–8 cm (2–3 in) in diameter. *N. mammulosus* is also an easy plant to grow. It has rather stouter, sharper, slightly flattened spines compared to *N. ottonis*. The flowers are yellow and bell-shaped. *N. concinnus* tends to

Above: ***Notocactus leninghausii*** **is a popular and widely cultivated species**

remain solitary and has long curly spines. The flowers are large – up to 10 cm (4 in) in diameter – and very freely produced. The more recently discovered *N. uebelmannianus* also usually remains solitary. The flowers are smaller, but in one form they can be a pink to purple.

A group of larger plants is sometimes placed into a separate genus, *Eriocactus.* *N. leninghausii* is a deservedly popular species, which is very commonly seen in cultivation. With golden spines and many ribs, it grows into a short columnar plant and branches from the base to form clumps. This plant must be a little larger than other notocacti before it flowers; the flowers are usually produced in big bunches from the tops of the stems, are relatively long lasting and, quite unusually, stay open at night. *N. leninghausii*, like a few other plants from this group, has a tendency to grow with the top on a slant. *N. magnificus*, a recently described species related to *N. leninghausii*, has shorter broader stems with fewer deeper ribs and a bluish colour to the body. It also grows into quite large clumps and can make magnificent specimens.

At the other end of the scale is *N. rutilans*, which rarely exceeds 8 cm (3 in) in height and 5 cm (2 in) in diameter. It flowers when small; the pink flowers shade into yellow at the centre. *N. scopa* is another common species, which comes in a wide variety of spine colours. Most forms are solitary and usually have yellow flowers. A different type of plant is *N. haselbergii*; this is globular with dense glassy white spines and long-lasting red flowers. The similar yellow-spined *N. graessneri* has green flowers.

Opuntia

This is the largest genus of cacti and most widely dispersed, containing some 300 species growing from Canada to Patagonia and from the West Indies to the Galapagos Islands. The genus is diverse, and various attempts have been made to split it into smaller genera. Opuntias, particularly the prickly pears, have become widely naturalized in many areas and in some places have become a serious weed.

All the opuntias contain in their areoles small spines called glochids. These have minute barbs, which very easily become detached and embedded in the skin and can be very irritating, so care must be taken in handling these plants. Some species also have a barbed sheath over the spines, which can also be very painful. These factors tend to make this group of plants unpopular, which is a pity because there are some interesting forms and many have beautiful flowers. Some species become quite large, so, unless space is not a problem, concentrate on the smaller, slower growing species.

The flat-padded opuntias are the most familiar, and perhaps one of the most common in cultivation is *Opuntia microdasys*. This Mexican species has dense glochids but no spines. In the typical form the glochids are brown and the pads 5–8 cm (2–3 in) in diameter. The flowers are yellow.

Many opuntias are cultivated for the fruit, which can either be eaten directly or turned into jams or preserves. For this purpose various strains of relatively spineless opuntias have been developed. Some of these derive from *O. ficus-indica*. These tend to be too large and uninteresting for horticultural purposes.

A number of more attractive species come from southern USA. These include *O. violacea* with purplish pads, long black spines and yellow flowers with a red centre. Fairly similar is *O. chlorotica*, which grows somewhat larger and has slightly bluer pads. *O. basilaris* is a very desirable species, which grows in California and Arizona. It makes small clumps of pads that stay close to the ground. The pads are somewhat bluish, and the flowers are a lovely cerise pink. Do not keep it too warm in winter or it will not flower. In dry conditions it should be fairly hardy. Another plant with a similar habit is *O. erinacea*; this has a dense covering of long white spines, and there are varieties with pink or yellow flowers. This one will withstand even colder conditions. Some opuntias grow in the far north of the USA, such as *O. polyacantha*. They are mostly low-growing plants, which stay close to the ground and are hardy even in the most extreme conditions.

Mexico has many species of flat-padded opuntias including perhaps one of the largest, the padded *O. robusta*. This can make pads some 45 cm (18 in) in diameter and gets to be a very large plant, so is suitable for cultivation only if you have plenty of space and can perhaps give it a free root run. The pads are also a nice glaucous blue colour.

Below: ***Opuntia ficus-indica*** **in cultivation showing the size to which it will grow**

Above: ***Opuntia vestita*** **in a group of cylindrical species from South America**

O. stenopetala is also an interesting species, which produces a lateral series of pads running across the ground, rooting as they go. It produces large numbers of small red to orange flowers. Other Mexican species commonly seen in cultivation include *O. pailana*, which is very spiny and gets quite tall, and *O. scheeri*, which has wispy spines that also occur on the flower buds and fruit. Another popular species is *O. pycnantha* from Baja California. This species is relatively slow growing and needs more cautious watering. Its flowers are relatively small and yellow.

Flat-padded opuntias are not confined to North and Central America. A very interesting large-growing species occurs on the Galapagos Islands. *O. galapagia* grows a massive spiny trunk and a big canopy of branches. *O. brasiliensis* also develops a large, woody, central trunk and has small, thin laterals which are shed after a few years. This species has small yellow flowers. A further interesting group of small, flat-padded opuntias comes from Argentina. These have pads no more than 5 cm (2 in) long and spread sideways across the ground. They flower quite easily and most, such as *O. erectoclada*, have quite large red flowers.

A very different group of opuntias are the chollas, which grow in northern Mexico and southern USA. These plants have woody, cylindrical stems that are very spiny, and they do not grow well in cultivation unless given very sunny conditions and a lot of space. *O. bigelowii* and *O. tunicata* may look attractive from a distance, but it is not advisable to get too close to them. There is a group of lower growing opuntias with small, club-shaped stems. Some of them are worth growing because they have interesting spines and some will flower when not too large. *O. invicta* has very strong spines, usually red when young. It is the largest of this group but relatively slow growing. The smallest, *O. planibulbispina*, has joints less than 2.5 cm (1 in) in length and small, dagger-like, white spines.

The cylindrical opuntias from South America are rather different. Some of the species, such as *O. subulata*, have large leaves and can be very rampant in growth. But the group also contains some choice, slower growing species, such as *O. pachypus*, which will not grow more than 5–8 cm (2–3 in) a year. The group also

Below: **The yellow form of** ***Opuntia microdasys*** **has the annoying habit of shedding pads in winter; the form with the white glochids flowers more easily**

Above: ***Opuntia galapageia*****, showing a close-up of the areoles and glochids, which are a marvellous golden-yellow becoming denser with age**

contains one or two fairly low-growing, high-altitude plants that are relatively hardy, such as *O. verschaffeldtii*, with pleasing red flowers, and *O. vestita* with its dense covering of wide hairs. *O. salmiana* is perhaps the easiest of opuntias to flower and is very abundant. It falls to pieces at the slightest touch, each joint rooting and forming new plants.

A number of South American opuntias are sometimes put in the genus *Tephrocactus*. They have globular joints and are relatively slow growing. Mostly high-altitude plants, they need very good light and can be somewhat reluctant to flower.

Oreocereus

Oreocereus are frequently seen in cultivation because of their attractive long white hairs. They come from high parts of the Andes in Peru and Bolivia and appreciate very good light. Known as the old man of the Andes, these plants can eventually reach 1.2 m (4 ft) or so in height and have a few dozen stems, but they are quite slow growing, and such plants must be many years old. However, they are very tough plants and are not difficult to grow. Do not expect flowers in cultivation unless conditions are exceptionally good.

Most common is *Oreocereus celsianus*, which develops long hairs and very sharp spines. Even slower and more densely woolly is *O. trollii*. There are some less attractive, faster growing species with less wool, such as *O. fossulatus*. They are a little more inclined to flower in cultivation. The flowers vary from pink through to a reddish-brown and are zygomorphic, like those of the matucanas.

Pachycereus

Another genus of cerei, *Pachycereus*, includes some of the largest cacti. The most commonly seen is *Pachycereus pringlei*, which comes from Baja California and adjacent areas on the mainland of Mexico. Seedlings are produced in large numbers by the wholesale cactus growers, and the species is commonly seen on sale in garden centres. It is quite easy to grow and makes a handsome pot plant.

For optimum growth it requires a large pot or free root run and good sunny conditions. This plant can eventually reach nearly 12 m (40 ft) in height, but such plants are a very great age. Other species of *Pachycereus*, such as *P. weberi*, come from somewhat further south in Mexico and are a bit more fussy about being

Below: This cholla opuntia is really too dangerous to have in an average collection

Above: ***Parodia chrysacanthion*** **has ring after ring of golden yellow flowers**

kept warm. *P. weberi* is a contender for the title of 'largest cactus' because, although it might not grow quite so tall, it forms a massive candelabra of branches.

Parodia

These cacti are from Argentina and Bolivia. They are globular to short cylindrical and produce good displays of flowers when quite small. Their roots are often a little on the weak side, so it is important not to let the soil become too alkaline with a build-up of salts. Many of the species have hooked spines, but there are exceptions, such as the golden-spined *Parodia chrysacanthion* with yellow flowers. The hooked-spined species may have yellow (*P. aureispina*) or red (*P. sanguiniflora*) flowers. There are many larger growing species with long hooked spines, such as *P. maassii*.

These have fairly small flowers. A few species, such as *P. marnieriana*, will offset to form clumps. This has rather small orange-red flowers. Many species, such as *P. schwebsiana*, produce much white wool from the new growth.

Pilosocereus

The genus *Pilosocereus* is a widespread group of columnar cacti, formerly included in the genus *Cephalocereus*. They come from Mexico, the West Indies and northern South America, but the largest number of species is found in Brazil. Although relatively large-growing plants, they are commonly cultivated because they have attractive coloured stems. The wholesale cactus nurseries produce large numbers of *Pilosocereus* because they are easy to grow from seed and make eye-catching plants.

P. palmeri is the species that has been in common cultivation for many years. It originates in Mexico. Although it eventually reaches around 4.5 m (15 ft) in height, it starts flowering at a manageable 1–1.2 m (3–4 ft). The stem colour varies from green to a slaty blue in some forms. The flower is nocturnal, pink and about 8 cm (3 in) in diameter. The areoles have a small amount of wool except those that bear the flowers, and these have a much denser woolly covering – a characteristic of the genus. There are a number of other species from Mexico, but the names reflect a certain amount of confusion. One other species that can be easily identified, however, is *P. chrysacanthus* with a covering of golden-yellow spines. They will grow quite quickly given generous-sized pots or a free root run.

A number of species come from the West Indies. They are quite fast growing and will make attractive plants, but they do need more heat than the Mexican species. Both *P. nobilis* and *P. barbadensis* are seen from time to time.

The Venezuelan species also need very warm conditions, but there are some attractive plants, including the recently described *P. tillianus* with long fine golden spines.

The Brazilian species used to be rare in cultivation but are now grown in huge numbers for the wholesale market. Some species have bright blue stems, the colour caused by a waxy covering on the epidermis. This persists for quite a few years, but eventually wears off with age.

Above: ***Pilosocereus glaucescens*****, from Brazil, showing the beginnings of a lovely blue stem**

Although these plants like greater warmth than most cacti, they are not as fussy as the West Indian species and are quite robust and easy to grow. They are fast growing, and many flower at a surprisingly small size, perhaps around 60 cm (2 ft) in height. The flowers are white, nocturnal and have an unpleasant, sickly smell that attracts the bats and moths that pollinate them in the wild. The fruits are quite large and have deep red flesh, which, when split open, creates an intense contrast against the blue stem.

Recommended species include *P. pentaedrophorus* with thin, five-angled, blue stems and small flowers, *P. magnificus* with thicker, intense blue stems with more ribs, *P. fulvilanatus* with five-angled thick stems and long golden hairs in the flowering areoles and *P. chrysostele* with more ribs and dense golden-yellow spines.

Rebutia

The genus *Rebutia* contains species that are ideal for the novice grower of cacti. They are very easy to grow and many species will flower by the time they are two years old in conditions no more demanding than a sunny windowsill. They flower in spring, from around the base of the plants, and there is a good range of flower colours, from reds to pinks to yellows. Some species can grow into quite large clumps and produce many hundreds of flowers each year. Some of the species have become hybridized as they readily set seed in cultivation. The commoner species include *Rebutia senilis* with white spines and usually red flowers, *R. marsoneri* with yellow flowers and *R. minuscula* with red to pink flowers.

Easily recognizable varieties are *R. fiebrigii* with rather longer spines and orange flowers and *R. krainziana* which has red flowers and very short white spines. *R. heliosa*, a relatively recent discovery, is smaller and has very tight pectinate spines. It is a little more difficult to grow than *R. krainziana* and should be watered rather more sparingly or put in a slightly more porous compost. *R. muscula* is also a little more difficult than the average rebutia; this species has dense white spines and orange flowers. Another relatively new species is *R. perplexa*, which has fairly small heads and pale pink flowers.

R. pygmaea comes from a slightly different group of rebutias. This is slower growing, has salmon-pink flowers and is very susceptible to attack by red spider mite.

Rhipsalis

This group of epiphytic cacti, mainly from Brazil, likes the same conditions as orchids and bromeliads. The soil should be acidic and peat based, and the plants should not be given prolonged dry spells. Frequent mist spraying of the stems is beneficial. Under these conditions they are easy to grow and make ideal hanging-basket plants. They are very suitable for indoor cultivation, but unfortunately seem to be available only through specialist nurseries.

The flowers are small and mostly white but are borne in great profusion, sometimes several from each areole, an unusual feature for cacti. There are quite a large number of species varying greatly in stem shape from broad, flattened stems to thin, cylindrical ones.

Commonly grown species include *Rhipsalis mesembryanthoides* with thin cylindrical stems, *R. pentaptera* with thicker, five-angled, winged stems, *R. crispimarginata* with broad, flat, wavy stems and *R. houletiana* with flat, slightly bluish stems.

Above: A display of mixed schlumbergera (Christmas cacti)

Schlumbergera

This genus includes the well-known Christmas cactus. This is not actually a species but a hybrid of horticultural origin. Most plants now sold as Christmas cacti have a slightly different parentage and also have a wider range of flower colours. The newer forms often flower slightly before Christmas; the older hybrids usually did not flower at Christmas, but more frequently in mid to late winter. The flowering of Christmas cacti is triggered by the shortening day length, and it is important not to disrupt this with too much artificial light. Like the rhipsalis, they are jungle cacti and need acidic, peat-based soils, no long dry periods and regular misting to create a humid atmosphere. The plants can eventually become quite large and put on very impressive flowering displays with hundreds of flowers out at once. The traditional Christmas cactus has magenta-pink flowers, but newer forms have been developed with many variations. There is a pure white form, but it will nevertheless show traces of pink in the flowers unless kept fairly warm.

There are some related species that flower later in the year. *Schlumbergera gaetneri*, the Easter cactus, has smaller scarlet flowers. Christmas cacti are sometimes grafted on a strong-growing cereus to produce a 'standard', which can produce a spectacular plant.

Stenocactus

This group, which is also known as *Echinofossulocactus*, comes from northern Mexico. They are characterized by having globular bodies with large numbers of wavy ribs, mostly flattened spines and small, striped flowers. They are related to the ferocacti but mostly stay much smaller.

The species are rather variable and difficult to distinguish. *Stenocactus albatus* has small, yellowish flowers and yellow to white spines. *S. crispatus* has longer spines and pink striped flowers. *S. coptonogonus* is unusual in having a small number of straight ribs.

Below: A young stenocactus exhibiting the characteristic wavy multi-ribbing

Stenocereus

From Mexico and the USA comes a group of large tree-like cacti. Because they are easy to grow from seed and have attractively marked stems as young seedlings, they are popular with wholesale cactus growers. To grow them to mature sizes, however, requires rather a lot of space and also quite warm conditions for some of the species.

Stenocereus thurberi, the organ-pipe cactus, is the only species that crosses the border into the USA. With brownish felted areoles it has an appeal but it is not too easy to grow in cultivation; like the *Carnegia*, which grows with it, it needs very hot sunny conditions. This plant can eventually reach 6 m (20 ft) in height. *S. pruinosus* and *S. chichipe* come from further south in Mexico, and, although faster growing, they may object to too cold conditions in winter. The chalky markings on their stems, prominent as seedlings, are not quite so pronounced in mature plants.

S. beneckei is perhaps the most suitable species for cultivation: it is smaller and shrubbier and the stems have a dense coating of white meal. Unfortunately, it is very sensitive to winter cold. The odd cactus known as the creeping devil, which originates in Baja California peninsula, is also usually placed here under modern classification. Its scientific name is *S. eruca* and it grows with the stems lying down on the ground, rooting into the sand as it grows. Eventually the older parts of the stem dry up, hence the epithet creeping. It can be grown in cultivation but its habit makes it awkward for pot cultivation, an open bed being more suitable.

Sulcorebutia

The sulcorebutias are high-altitude plants from Bolivia. They are relatively small and globular, forming small clumps. These plants are free flowering in cultivation given good light and are not particularly difficult to grow. There is a bewildering variety of intense flower colours, including some bicoloured forms. A common characteristic is the elongated rather than circular areole.

All the species are worth growing, and among those most commonly seen are *Sulcorebutia candiae*, which is one of the larger-growing species with golden spines and yellow flowers, *S. steinbachii* with red or pinkish flowers, *S. glomeriseta* with dense white spines and yellow flowers, *S. caniguerallii* with bicoloured flowers – orange with a yellow centre – and *S. arenacea* with neat, symmetrical spination and yellow flowers.

Above: ***Thelocactus lloydii*, which prefers a clay half-pot and a high mineral content to the soil, will reward you with shining deep pink and red flowers**

Thelocactus

This group of very spiny, globular cacti comes from northern Mexico and the southern USA. Under good sunny conditions they produce large, showy flowers. On the whole they prefer a well-drained, mineral-based compost. *Thelocactus bicolor* is a very widespread species of which there are a large number of forms, all differing in size, shape and spine colour. All have pink flowers 8–10 cm (3–4 in) in diameter with a deeper red mid-stripe in the centre and of a very glossy texture. They are fairly slow growing, needing less than average water. *T. hexaedrophorus* has a more open, flatter body and pure white flowers. There are some slightly larger growing species, such as *T. lophothele*, which have prominently tubercled bodies and long spines. Their flowers are yellow to pale pink. *T. lloydii* is a plant somewhat allied to *T. bicolor*; it has similar flowers but a much more open flattened body and very strong spines.

Trichocereus

This is a group of large columnar cacti from Argentina, Chile and Bolivia. The smaller sizes are sometimes included in the genus *Echinopsis*. They have similar, large, mostly white, nocturnal flowers and are very vigorous plants frequently used as stocks for grafting; if adequate space is available they are well worth growing for their own merits. Some of the lower-growing clumping varieties flower at the smallest sizes. Typical is *T. schickendantzii* with 25 cm (10 in) diameter pure white flowers. *T. candicans*, which comes in a wide variety of forms, has short, thick stems.

Below: ***Trichocereus candicans*** **showing the multitude of heads this species acquires with age. The heads on this plant are 15 cm (6 in) across and up to 45 cm (18 in) long**

The species from Chile, *T. chilensis*, has very strong spines and is somewhat slower growing and more reluctant to flower. *T. macrogonus* is much taller growing with slightly blue stems. It needs to be around 1.8 m (6 ft) or more to flower but can reach this height very quickly under favourable conditions.

The real giants of the genus can get to 9 m (30 ft) or more and 60 cm (2 ft) in diameter. They are slower growing but a good deal faster than their North American counterparts. *T. pasacana* and *T. terscheckii* are in this group.

Some *Trichocereus* with coloured flowers are classified in the genus *Lobivia*. They are smaller and will flower at manageable sizes. *T. huascha* and *T. grandiflora*, usually with red flowers, belong to this group.

Turbinicarpus

This is a genus of rather rare miniature cacti from Mexico. They are quite slow growing but on the whole not particularly difficult if treated with care. Seedlings are readily available from specialist nurseries, and they start flowering at quite small sizes. As they develop into small clumps they are probably best grown in clay pots and a fairly mineral-based soil for safety. All species are worth growing, but *Turbinicarpus lophophoroides* is a little more temperamental than most.

Uebelamannia

This unusual genus of just a few species is from the hot, dry areas of northeast Brazil. These plants are difficult in cultivation and are frequently grown grafted. They have unusual gum cells in the epidermis which make it glisten. The flowers are small and insignificant.

Succulents

Adenium (Apocynaceae)

This increasingly popular genus of succulent plants comes from Africa and southern Arabia. The common names are desert rose, impala lily, mock azalea, desert azalea and sabi star – for the simple reason that this plant has beautiful, showy flowers and masses of them when the growing conditions are right.

Coming from these hot areas, it needs well-drained compost and extra heat in winter. This is a very good houseplant subject and looks good in a blue-and-white Chinese pot. The plants are usually multi-branched and in the wild can achieve heights of 3 m (10 ft), when they have great swollen trunks, like huge rocks sitting in the desert. They flower at a relatively young age depending on the conditions, possibly within two years from seed, but more usually within about three to four years.

Most widely available is *Adenium obesum*, from Tanzania and Natal. The five-petalled flowers are pink, but some varieties have white flowers. The horticultural trade is currently developing plants with larger flowers, so watch out for these in the future.

Propagation is usually from seed, but cuttings may be taken to salvage a plant that is rotting.

Adromischus (Crassulaceae)

Adromischus are attractive, small, low-growing, leaf succulents, which are closely related to the genus *Cotyledon*. They are not in the least bit hardy away from their native South Africa and Namibia, but they can be grown out of doors, in pots during the frost-free months of the year, slugs and snails willing. Many of the species have intense red-brown markings or patterns on the leaves, which are intensified by good light. Some species also have textured leaves, like *Adromischus marianae*; others have leaf edges that are crinkled or wavy, such as *A. cristatus*; yet others, like *A. leucophyllus*, have a white coating to the leaves, a farina; this makes them less suitable for the open air as this farina can be washed off in heavy rains.

Cultivation is simple, for they grow readily from leaves set in sandy soil. No two plants seem to be exactly the same, for the markings are unique to each plant, unless they are produced from leaves from the same parent. The small pink or white flowers are set close to the stem. *A. grandiflora*, as the name suggests, has the largest flowers.

Aeonium (Crassulaceae)

This fairly small genus of usually monocarpic plants is from the Canary Islands, Cape Verde Islands, Madeira and North Africa. They are often seen in garden centres, particularly the plants with dark maroon leaves. Among these are *Aeonium arboreum* 'Atropurpureum' and *A.* 'Schwarzkopf', which is even darker and more vigorous. These plants are useful for summer bedding, but need to be lifted, potted and given protection before any frosts arrive.

The growth habit for these plants is a tall, naked stem, often over 45 cm (18 in), topped

Below: ***Adromischus marianae*** **var.** ***herreri***

Above: ***Agave victoria-reginae*** **from Nuevo-Leon in Mexico makes large handsome specimens**

with a rosette of leaves, which may be shiny or matt, and occasionally hairy (*A. smithii* and *A. simsii*), with an inflorescence. Luckily, before it flowers the plant has usually had several sideshoots, so all is not lost; additionally, the plant may set seed. The flowers are usually yellow, occasionally white or pink (*A. nobile*), and the inflorescence will have upwards of a hundred small flowers arranged pyramidically, with the flowers opening in succession over a long period.

One species, *A. tabuliforme*, does not have shoots, but grows flush with the ground often attaining, in cultivation, the size of a dinner plate. Cultivation for this species is from seed or occasionally from leaves. A cristate or monstrose form of this is more often available; by taking the small individual heads off this, normal plants can sometimes be grown.

Agave (Agavaceae)

These highly architectural, rosette-forming, mostly stemless, succulents are found on the North American continent and offshore islands. Most species have a sharp spine at the tips of the leaves, and on many species there is a series of sharp teeth along the outer leaf margins. These are saw-like and can cause a nasty tear if handled roughly. The plants range from 15 cm (6 in) to 5 m (16 ft). Some species will tolerate quite cold conditions but will need extra drainage if planted in the open ground. Plant the rosettes at an angle so that moisture does not collect in the centre and can drain away quickly.

The most commonly encountered species is *Agave americana* and its varieties, including *A. americana* 'Variegata' (yellow stripe down the leaf margins) and *A. americana* 'Mediopicta' (white stripe in the middle of the leaf, running from tip to base). The last is usually the most expensive, being a little slower to make a large specimen. None of these three is totally hardy; the first two may survive some winters unharmed, but a bad winter will kill them if they are not protected from the elements. *A. victoria-reginae*, from Mexico, is a handsome species with many white lines on the leaves; these lines are formed while the new leaves are compacted at the centre of the plant and as the leaves open out the white lines are left behind. *A. parviflora* has the same characteristic, but additionally has curling white filaments at the leaf edges.

Agaves with blue or fairly thin leaves are the most likely to be cold tolerant, while the fatter and paler green-leaved species are likely to come from a warmer environment.

The common name for these plants is century agave. This is a misnomer, as most species flower long before they are a hundred years old. However, they do have to 'gather' themselves for the effort of flowering, and after they flower the rosette dies. Hopefully, during its lifetime the agave will have produced some offsets, or seeds from which new plants may be grown. It is important to pot on the larger growing species regularly to enable them to attain their true potential, but this can be a hazardous experience. It can also be difficult to find a movable pot that is large enough.

Aichryson (Crassulaceae)

Aichrysons are mostly biennial plants. Although they are loosely related to aeoniums, they are very much smaller, hairy-leaved cousins from the Canary Islands off the west coast of Africa. These yellow-flowered plants may be grown out of doors, but only in the most sheltered of places.

They are summer flowering and do well if allowed to stand out of doors for the warmer months, then taken in under cover before a frost. They are mostly monocarpic but luckily are self-fertile, producing masses of small seed, which scatters everywhere, germinating like mustard and cress. Once this plant has been acquired, it is most unlikely to leave you.

Above: ***Aloe pratensis*** **is a smaller growing species from South Africa**

Aloe (Asphodelaceae)

Aloes belong to a very large family containing some 300 genera and 4,500 species. The genera that are closely related to *Aloe* and are widely grown are *Bulbine, Bowiea, Ornithogalum* (the last two not considered succulent by some experts), *Haworthia, Astroloba, Lomatophyllum* and *Gasteria*. The aloes are found naturally on the African continent, in Madagascar and the Arabian peninsula. Like the agaves, some of the aloes, *Aloe vera*, for example, have been collected by travellers and distributed to all parts of the globe. *A. vera* is found in so many locations that its original habitat is not known.

These plants are often confused with agaves, and in part this must be due to the teeth that many of the aloes have, although these are usually much softer and do not normally cause damage. Like the agaves, they mostly grow in rosettes, but sometimes this characteristic is not that evident and it may only happen with age. Unlike agaves, they are not monocarpic and should, once they start, flower annually; the flower will sometimes lead to the plant branching dichotomously. The flower spike, which may be simple or branched, often comes from a little way out of the centre of the plant. The flower colours range from white through yellow and orange to red, and some even have green flowers. Many of the aloes want to grow in the winter months in the

Below: Aichrysons are short-lived succulents that grow very easily from seed

northern hemisphere, which means that they will have to be given some water during the coldest months.

Aloes come in a variety of sizes, ranging from 2.5 cm (1 in) to 18 m (58 ft) in height, and can have stems or trunks of up to 3 m (10 ft), so it is important to select the right one for your conditions.

The most common species offered for sale is *A. aristata*. Do not discard this as not worth growing: it flowers most reliably and is very generous with its offsets, making it an ideal plant to propagate for fund-raising events. This is one of the hardiest of the aloes and will tolerate being grown out of doors in the south of Britain, provided the soil is well drained and the plant is protected from the very worst of the winter weather.

A. variegata (partridge breast aloe) must be the second most commonly grown of this genus; it seems to be particularly well suited to windowsill cultivation and enjoys being pot-bound and baked by the sun. Because it will not be potted on so regularly it needs to be watered and fed during the winter, otherwise it will not produce its very lovely flower spikes in early spring. It produces offsets with age and these can be removed and grown on in separate pots. This species can be grown out of doors all the year round, but always in a very dry spot.

Above: ***Aloe ericacea*** **is a slow-growing, xerophytic species**

Two very statuesque aloes which may appear in your local garden centre or nursery are *A. dichotoma* and *A. pillansii*. These are tree aloes, which have very thick trunks and can attain the height of small trees. *A. pillansii* is an endangered species in the wild with only a few specimens left and no regeneration. This sorry plight has probably been caused by overgrazing and possibly collecting; however, other factors such as changing climate may be playing a part. *A. dichotoma*, on the other hand, is very common in the wild and in many areas is the only 'tree' to be seen. It is used by the sociable weaver birds to house their huge communal nests.

In cultivation this plant must be potted-on regularly if it is to grow well; a deficiency in either food or water will result in the leaves dying back from the tips.

Below: The attractive leaf colour of ***Aloe gariepensis*** **in its natural habitat**

Above: ***Aloe melanocantha*** **is a very attractive slow-growing species**

A. plicatilis is another tree aloe, and although this species does not attain the same proportions as the previous two, neither does it grow so rapidly. It will, on the other hand, flower at a much younger age, even when grown in a pot. Winter growing and flowering in the northern hemisphere, this strap-leaf aloe branches both before and with flowering. It is one of the few aloes that does not form a rosette of leaves.

A. jucunda, from Somalia, is a small-headed, spotted aloe which clumps with age into a plant 0.6–1 m (2–3 ft) across if you wish. It offsets freely, so there is no problem keeping this plant to the proportions you can accommodate; the offsets that have been removed can then be potted up and passed on to friends. This plant flowers freely and many times during the summer months in the northern hemisphere, only ceasing when the light levels drop too low. It is a very glossy-leaved species with fairly hard teeth along the leaf margins. Hybrids are available because it has been crossed with *A. haworthioides*, *A. belatula* and *A. rauhii*, to name but three. Other aloes in this group that are equally worthwhile growing are *A. peckii*, *A. somaliensis*, *A. kingiana*, *A. mcloughlanii* and *A. hemmingsii*. Most are considerably large.

A. erinacea, *A. pachygaster* and *A. melanacantha* are all desirable species to grow, the last reaching the largest proportions. *A. melanacantha* has leaves with a very rough surface, with strong, black teeth or spines along the leaf margins. These spines are pale yellow and soft when the leaves first emerge from the centre of the plant, but they harden and darken as they mature. *A. erinacea* and *A. pachygaster* are Namibian species, whereas *A. melanacantha* occurs up the west coast of South Africa and just into Namibia. *A. erinacea* and *A. pachygaster* have a beautiful blue appearance to the leaves and again the strong, dark spines.

These plants do not take kindly to being overwatered and require full sun.

Below: ***Aloe striata*** **has one of the more attractive infloresences in the genus**

Above: ***Ceropegia ampliata*** **is a large-flowered, vining species which flowers late in the year**

Aloinopsis (Aizoaceae)

These little plants are native to Cape Province of South Africa. They are low growing, without stems above ground, but have a thickened or swollen stem or rootstock below ground. The leaves are light grey, grey-brown or green; many but not all species have tubercles and some appear toothed. The flowers are either yellow, yellow with a red mid-stripe or pink.

Three of the species, *Aloinopsis rosulata*, *A. rubrolineata* and *A. schooneesii*, have a similar epidermis, reminiscent of a lizard's skin. *A. schooneesii* has a very large, tuberous rootstock compared with the amount of growth above ground, like an iceberg: 10 per cent above ground and 90 per cent below ground.

A. spathulata, the only species with pink flowers, has greyish-pink, spathulate leaves. Extra drainage is recommended for this species, which grows from late summer to winter.

Propagation is from seed; although they can be rooted from cuttings this is usually only done to rescue a plant that would otherwise die.

Other closely related genera requiring similar treatment are *Delianthe*, *Nananthus*, *Rabiea* and *Titanopsis* (see page 115).

Ceropegia (Asclepiadaceae)

Ceropegia is a large genus of about 150 species, which grow in the wild from Africa to the Far East. They are mostly vining, twining plants, although several species on the Canary Islands (*Ceropegia fusca*, *C. dichotoma* and *C. hians*) have taken succulence a degree further by developing fatter, jointed stems and not vining. A few species have evolved their method of water storage in the other direction by developing underground tubers.

With a few exceptions these are fairly easy plants to grow and respond well to being grown in captivity, whether in a greenhouse or conservatory or indoors. *C. woodii*, often sold in garden centres and flower shops, makes a good hanging-basket plant, having little purple, green and grey heart-shaped leaves. Often the hanging, vining stems make aerial tubers, which can be taken off with a little of the vine attached and rooted to make further plants. The flowers are always upward turned, and are like little, inverted parachutes; the petals are united for most of their length, only parted for the last 20 per cent, but often rejoined again at the very tip: the pollinators have got to be able to get into the flower to do their job.

C. ampliata is a large-flowered, vining species, which is thoroughly recommended. Flowering takes place rather late in the year. The flowers are mostly white with green tips to the petals. *C. haygarthii* is another popular vining species from the eastern Transvaal, which has medium-sized, flat-topped parachute flowers. *C. sandersonii* is similar but has much larger flowers.

One quite common but very different species is *C. stapeliiformis* from East Cape Province. The stems on this plant may be upright when very young but it soon falls over and starts clambering up whatever is available. The stems are mottled brown and grey and get very thin as the plant prepares to flower. This is a robust species, but a little brittle at times, so plenty of cuttings are usually available.

There are more species that could be recommended; most are relatively easy. Propagation is by cuttings or from seed.

Conophytum (Aizoaceae)

Conophytums come from southern Africa and Namibia, often growing on quartz patches of ground, in depressions in rocks and in rock crevices. They have taken leaf succulence a degree further than lithops: what were the upper sides of flat leaves are almost totally united. Only a small slit remains to denote that each head is formed from two leaves. Some conophytum leaves are not so united, and these are referred to as bilobes because they have two distinct leaves, which are usually united for half their length.

In the 1990s a complete revision of this group of plants took place and *Conophytum* now includes *Conophytum*, *Berrisfordia*, *Herreanthus* and *Ophthalmophyllum*.

Below: ***Conophytum spectabile*** **is heavily scented**

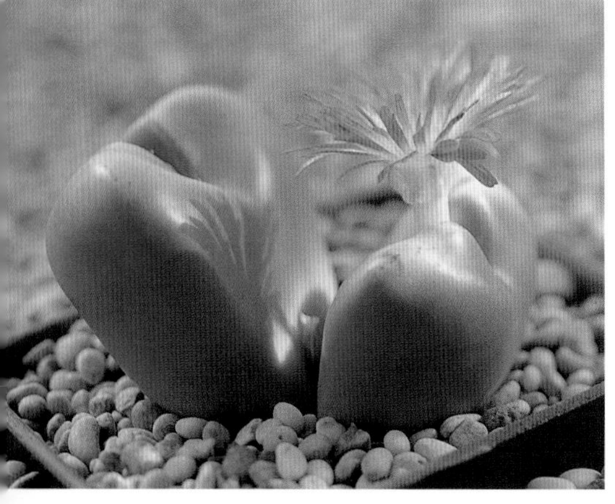

Above: ***Conophytum lithopsoides*****, a soft-bodied plant, flowering profusely in early autumn**

Conophytums are perhaps easier to grow than lithops; they are less likely to rot through overwatering or being left in unfavourable conditions. Their growing and resting periods are slightly different from lithops; in the northern hemisphere conophytums need to be rested for the first six months of the year, with one watering in early spring. They have to go through the same process as lithops: the production of a new leaf pair and the reduction of the previous leaf pair by absorbence by the new heads. During the resting period it is advisable to take conophytums out of direct sunlight, perhaps placing them under the bench in a greenhouse, otherwise they may get too hot and cook in their resting bodies. Once they start to grow again in midsummer they must be brought into good light again.

The individual leaf pair of a conophytum is called a head. These heads are usually much smaller than those of lithops: in some species they are not much bigger than a matchstick head, while in others they may be 6.5 cm (2½ in) long. They are usually a shade of green and often spotted. The bilobes and other keeled species often have a red margin running along the keel. There is often a thin, darker green line surrounding the fissure, which is a small window.

Conophytums are quite capable of producing between three and seven new heads from the previous year's single head. This will depend on the species; the bilobes, being somewhat larger, are the types likely to generate the most heads. It does mean that a large mound of heads can be achieved in a relatively short time. It is important to keep the old leaf litter tidied away from the new heads, although this can be a tedious pastime. As you may imagine, these little heads afford many nooks and crannies in which pests can multiply.

These little jewels are propagated either by seed sown in a sandy loam and not covered, or by taking cuttings after the resting period. Each individual head can be made into a cutting and should root within 14 days, if the soil is kept slightly moist. Mist spraying the cuttings and seedlings is a good idea as it avoids the soil becoming too waterlogged.

These enchanting little gems can flower within one to two years of the seed being sown and the blooms are really worth waiting for. The flower colours range from white to cream to pink to magenta, to purple, to yellow, orange and red or mahogany. Not only do conophytums have a much greater flower colour range than lithops, but unlike lithops there are nocturnal-flowering species. Lithops flowers tend to have much thinner petals and are usually a straw colour, but a few have pink flowers. One advantage the nocturnal-flowering species have over the other species is the very strong and exquisite perfume they exude. This attracts nocturnal pollinators, moths probably, which rely on their sense of smell rather than sight to direct them to their food sources.

Below: ***Conophytum*** **x 'Shukuden'**

Recommended day-flowering species are *Conophytum wettsteinii* with relatively large, flat-topped, pale green, unspotted heads and purple flowers; *C. taylorianum* with green, keeled, spotted heads and pale purple flowers; and *C. bilobum* with two distinct lobed leaves to each head, unspotted, sometimes with a red keel, and yellow flowers. *C. frutescens* is another bilobed species with slightly thinner leaves and orange flowers. *C. incurvum* var. *leucanthum* completes the trio, as this is another bilobe, but this time with white flowers. *C. globosum* is, as the name suggests, round headed and spotted and has pale purple flowers. *C.* x *marnierianum* is a very easily grown plant, a naturally and unnaturally occurring hybrid, which is quite variable in its body markings and flower colours, which range from yellow through orange to purple. *C. ectypum* var. *tischleri* is a lovely species with large golden flowers. *C. pellucidum* has a multitude of forms with no two plants being identical, but it is the flowers that really put the icing on top of the cake as they are a pristine white with a small egg-yolk yellow centre; a few forms have pale pink-purple flowers. This last species, *C. pellucidum*, is one to acquire once some of the others have been mastered.

Of the nocturnal-flowering species the following are recommended. *C. spectabile* with a darkish green body with irregular red lines and spots on the upper parts and medium-purple flowers with a heavenly perfume; the flat-topped *C. obcordellum* var. *ceresianum*

Above: ***Conophytum*** **x** ***marnierianum*** **is a naturally occurring hybrid of** ***C. bilobum*** **and** ***C. ectypum***

with some red spots and lines and a pale pink flower; *C. truncatum* with a larger head than either of the previous two species, slightly spotted and with straw-coloured, scented flowers.

The popularity of these plants in Japan has led to the widespread hybridization of a number of the species. These are inter-generic hybrids with Anglicized Japanese names, which are variously mis-spelled. Often orange-flowered plants are produced by hybridizing yellow- and purple-flowered species, but this is not always the case. Another characteristic that has been developed in the hybrids is a whorling of the flowers, so that they resemble a catherine wheel.

These recommendations will get you started on the road to growing this charming group of plants, and as your interest deepens you will find it helpful to contact specialist nurseries and groups.

Cotyledon (Crassulaceae)

This small genus of around ten species originates mostly in southern Africa. Winter growing and flowering, these plants can have hairy or smooth leaves, round or pointed, disc shaped or egg shaped. Often the plants are quite variable within one species and may sometimes have plain green leaves, whitish leaves (with a farina) and may have a red margin around the leaves.

One of the smaller species and therefore suited to a small greenhouse or conservatory is *Cotyledon ladismithensis*. This is one of the hairy-leaved varieties and produces bell-shaped orange flowers quite easily. It forms a small, bushy plant and is easily propagated from cuttings. *C. eliseae* has only recently been named, having been around for a number of years as the 'cotyledon from Quartz River canyon'. Smaller than *C. ladismithensis*, it has glutinous hairs on the leaves, every particle of soil sticking to the leaves when it is being repotted. *C. eliseae* with deep orange flowers makes a suitable subject for a hanging basket.

C. orbiculata has many forms, most having a bluish-white appearance to the leaves with a red margin. There is a form around without the attractive hue to the leaves, but this is much less common. An attractive species to grow, it is easy to cultivate from cuttings or leaves; the

Below: ***Cotyledon ladismithensis*** **is one of the smaller species and is suitable for a small greenhouse or conservatory**

flowers are bell shaped with the tips of the orange petals splaying outwards.

Crassula (Crassulaceae)

This very large genus contains some 200 species coming from the southern hemisphere, predominantly South Africa, but found even in Australia and New Zealand. They are very variable plants, ranging from those that are hardy and suitable for the rock garden, the ground-hugging *Crassula sediforme*, to those that are aquatic, *C. helmsii*, and to plants such as *C. ovata* that can reach a height and width of up to 2.5 m (8 ft).

They are for the most part easy to grow and propagate, predominantly by cuttings, although they can be raised from seed, which is very fine. Many species like to grow and flower in the winter months in the northern hemisphere, but they still look quite attractive even when they are not in full growth. The following are plants that are easily located or that are well worth trying to find.

C. ovata has had a number of names and can still be found in garden centres and nurseries under most of them. *C. argentea* and *C. portulacea* are the other two Latin names often used, but there is also a range of common names, including tree of happiness, jade tree, money plant, penny plant and Chinese rubber plant. Its habitat is Natal and East Cape Province in South Africa.

C. ovata must be the most popular crassula, being propagated from cuttings very easily and frequently. It has glossy, dark evergreen leaves and sheds its oldest leaves when it is neglected for it needs to conserve moisture and food. It flowers, budding up in late autumn and opening the flowers in midwinter. The flowers are star-shaped, with white petals which have a tinge of pink; although the individual flowers are small, they are arranged in bunches all over the plant and can make quite a show. Much of the beauty of this plant lies in the massive tree-like trunk that it develops with age. It can be a problem finding a container large enough to accommodate this plant, but should it begin to get too large then it is easy to take a cutting and keep it in reserve against the day when the original plant becomes unmanageable.

These plants command very high prices in garden centres, sometimes surprisingly astronomical prices considering the rapidity with which they can grow if they are fed and watered continuously. Although *C. ovata* enjoys being taken out of doors in summer, it is not essential to do this to encourage flowering. However, the plant will keep a better shape if it is given maximum sunlight. As a houseplant *C. ovata* is often found growing in poor light and getting rather etiolated, until the distance between the leaf pairs becomes too great and the smaller branches begin to bend and look weak. This is not a subject for the bathroom, dark hall or similar place; it will not die if kept there but nor will it flourish and look robust. There are other forms with different leaf colours: 'Blue Haze' or 'Blue Bird' (blue leaved – not the same as *C. arborescens*) and 'Hummel's Sunset' which has gold and red colouring in the leaves that is really brought out in strong sunlight. Another cultivar is 'Crosby's Compact', which is similar to *C. ovata* but has smaller leaves and is slower to grow, although it still makes quite a large plant with age.

C. arborescens is very similar to *C. ovata*: it has the same mode of growth, although is not so fast growing. This plant comes from West Cape Province in South Africa, which is drier than the habitat of *C. ovata*. The main differences are the leaf colour, which is blue with a red margin, and the leaf shape, which is round, compared to the mostly ovate leaves of *C. ovata*. The leaves of *C. arborescens* are also thicker than those of *C.ovata*.

Above: **The delightful *Crassula nealeana* in flower**

The delightful little *C. nealeana* from South Africa first came to prominence in the early 1930s. It is unlikely to grow beyond a 11 cm (4½ in) pot but is easily pruned if it does get too big. Easy to cultivate from cuttings, this plant has small, bluish, opposite pairs of leaves with a red edge. It flowers in autumn producing a white, branched inflorescence; the backs of the petals are red.

At different times *C. arta* has been classified as *C. cornuta*, *C. deceptor*, or *C. deceptrix* and *C. deltoidea*. Whatever its name, it is a very attractive and small-growing species. Certainly all of the plants described under these names are closely related, and it may be that the variability between the named species is due to the different areas they come from, although all are from South Africa.

The habit of these little succulents is to stack their white, paired leaves alternately up a very short stem. The leaves are mostly spotted, but this is difficult to determine because of the very whiteness, which is a type of coating on the leaves, not a farina as it cannot be wiped off. Do not overwater these plants; they are slow growing and so need to dry out between waterings. Use a well-drained compost and postition them in good light.

Another crassula worthy of gracing a collection is *C. falcata*, formerly known as *Rochea falcata*. It is also known as *C. perfoliata* var. *minor*. It has rough, bluish-grey leaves, which look like aeroplane propellers; technically, the leaves are falcate or sickle shaped. This plant will reach 30–45 cm (12–18 in) in height, and will be even taller once it is in flower as the inflorescence rises a further 15–20 cm (6–8 in) above the leaves. The deep coral red flowerhead is quite large and as an added bonus is heavily and sweetly scented. Once the plant has flowered, it should shoot from the base and the top of the plant; at this point it may be better to start the plant again from a young shoot.

C. mesembryanthemopsis, rather a long name for a little plant, is so called because it resembles a mesembryanthemum. This is one of the smallest crassulas and also one of the most attractive. It has bluish-white, triangular leaves with flattened tips formed in a rosette, tightly hugging the ground. Whenever a plant hugs the ground, it is worth adding extra drainage material to the soil to combat the moisture that collects around the neck of the plants. To keep the leaves from having contact with the soil it is a good idea to put a layer of coarse sand or grit between the two. It grows in autumn–winter–spring, producing its flower clusters, which are white and sit in the centre of the rosette, in autumn.

C. x 'Morgan's Beauty' is a hybrid of *C. falcata* and *C. mesembryanthemopsis*, and it has somehow managed to select the best characteristics of both parents. It has the bluish-grey rough leaves of *C. falcata* but the compact habit of *C. mesembryanthemopsis*. When it flowers it falls midway between the two, having a pink cluster of highly scented flowers in the centre of each head or rosette. This is an absolute 'must have'.

C. nemorosa, which is native to South West Cape Province in South Africa, is an unusual little crassula. It grows from tiny underground tubers and in late summer to early autumn these tubers send up small, bluish-grey stems with small, heart-shaped leaves. During the late autumn, if the plants are watered enough, the stems produce relatively large, bell-shaped, creamy-white flowers. It is important that these plants are allowed to rest during the summer; during this time all the topgrowth dies down. Doubtless many pots of these tubers have been discarded as the owners believed them to be dead, when the tubers were, in fact, merely resting.

Repotting *C. nemorosa* can be a bit of a problem if it is undertaken while the plants are lying dormant. It is much better to do it when they are just into growth, or, failing that, just give them a good feed and forget about repotting the plants altogether. Propagation is from potting up the little tubers, which will multiply readily.

C. muscosa, which was formerly named *C. lycopodioides* and will still be found with that name, is another easily acquired plant. It comes from South West Africa and in many forms. Its more usual habit is a small bush with stems 20–40 cm (8–16 in) tall and 3–10 cm (1¼–4 in) in diameter – in other words, it is tall and skinny. The leaves are close packed round the stem, covering it completely, giving rise to its common name, lizard's tail. The flowers are yellow and so small that you may be forgiven for missing them if your plant has flowered, which it does in spring. However, there is a strange smell – it cannot be called a perfume – which the flowers exude when they are open. This is a very variable species. Some plants are so tiny that they really do resemble the patches of moss for which this plant is named. There are variegated forms as well as cristate and, more usually, monstrose forms. Cultivation is easy from cuttings.

Below: ***Crassula plegmatoides*** **on a rockery in South Africa with the quartz stones it would be growing near to in its natural habitat**

Both *C. marnierana* and *C. rupestris* are seen on offer quite frequently. Neither species is difficult to grow. Both are commonly called the jade necklace plant.

Some other recommended crassulas are *C. columnella*, *C. barklyi* (which was until recently known as *C. teres*), *C. pyramidalis* and *C. quadrangularis*, each of which has an upright habit, often only clumping with age, and having densely stacked pairs of leaves. When these plants flower that is the end of that particular head, so unless there are shoots at the base or adventitious shoots appear on the stem after flowering, the plant is lost. The flowers appear in tufts on the crown of the plant and are usually sweetly scented.

Further recommendations are *C. tecta* and *C. alstonii* (very choice). These plants produce flowers on longer flower spikes and they are held in bunches like a pompon. They are both whitish in appearance and do not like being overwatered.

Finally, there are three crassulas that make statuesque plants at up to 38 cm (15 in), without getting too tall. They are *C. conjuncta*, *C. sladeniana* and *C. perforata* and all are easily propagated from cuttings.

Dasylirion (Nolinaceae)

The plants in this small genus are capable of attaining diameters of 3–4 m (10–13 ft) in their natural habitat of southern USA and Mexico. Dioecious and monocarpic, like the agaves, these rosette-forming plants gather themselves for flowering then die after producing seed.

Dasylirion wheeleri is the most common species, with narrow, 60 cm (2 ft) long leaves, thin in cross-section. The leaves have fine teeth along the margins, which point towards the centre of the plant. The plume-like flower spike attains a height of 3 m (9 ft). The seeds are tightly packed in the pods and are small, black discs. As with the agaves, the seeds are often heavily parasitized in the wild by the very insects that help to pollinate them. Although it is tender, a well-grown mature plant will survive a degree or two of frost.

Above: ***Dasylirion wheeleri*, the most commonly grown species of this genus**

Dudleya (Crassulaceae)

These New World succulents come from California, Arizona and Mexico. Rosette forming and usually with farinose leaves, they are attractive plants. The leaves are easily marked, however, and once the white farina has been wiped or scraped off the leaf surface it will not regrow. The farina helps the plants retain moisture in their leaves and not lose it through evaporation. In the wild this farina will be partially dispersed by heavy rains, but these usually come when the plant is dormant and the rosettes are partly closed.

Dudleyas, unlike echeverias, do not shed their lower, dried-up leaves, but tend to hang on to them, perhaps as protection for the stem. They grow in summer and flower towards the end of it, bearing many small, greenish-yellow, star-shaped flowers on one or two long flower stems. The smaller the species the more flower stems it will have. These plants do not have to be kept particularly warm in winter, but do not like to get frosted. Individual dudleya rosettes can attain a diameter of 50 cm (20 in), although not all the species grow this large. *Dudleya brittonii* and *D. anthonyi* do get big. Usually they do not offset but have one very large head of leaves.

For the serious collector, the fat-leaved *D. pachyphytum* is a 'must-have' plant. It too has the white farina, with leaves as fat as fingers at times. It comes from Mexico and is particularly slow growing, whether from seed or from cuttings.

D. farinosa is one of the smaller growing species that are widely available. It has many small leaves 6 cm (2½ in) long and 2–3 cm (¾–1¼ in) broad. Other small-growing species recommended include *D. cymosa* and *D. saxosa*.

For something completely different try *D. viscida*; this plant has long narrow leaves, without the farina. Instead, it has a viscid or glutinous covering on the leaves, and all manner of small objects, from soil particles to small insects, become attached to the leaves and act as a protection in much the same way as the farina does for the other species.

Echeveria (Crassulaceae)

These members of the Crassulaceae are much more widely dispersed than are the former genera, but they are still New World succulents. Their range is from southern USA through Mexico and Central America down into Argentina. They are easy to cultivate, easy to hybridize and easy to propagate – a beginner's dream. Some of the plants are unkindly referred to by hardened cactophiles as 'cabbages' or 'Brussels sprouts'; indeed, some of the hybrids do have very large crinkly leaves.

These very accommodating plants are used in several ways: by local and borough councils in seaside towns as bedding plants; for summer planting in containers in the garden; planted through a chicken-wire shape to be suspended from a pergola or hanging-basket hook; and grown in pots in a greenhouse.

There are 100 to 150 species and a lot more hybrids. They can have plain green leaves, hairy leaves, purple leaves, blue leaves and, like the dudleyas, some even have a white farina. They are rosette forming and flower freely throughout the year, often sending up flower spikes more than once in the year. The flowers range from pure lemon-yellow through to bright scarlet, and many species have bi-coloured yellow and orange or yellow and red flowers.

New species of *Echeveria* are still being discovered; they cover such a wide area with high mountain chains that it is almost impossible for every nook and cranny to have been explored for plants. In addition, it usually takes time to establish whether a plant that has been found is new or merely a new location for an existing species.

Hybrids abound and are not usually grown for the flowers but for the leaf form or colour. Many have their origins in the USA and have been deliberately hybridized, although some must have happened spontaneously in enthusiasts' collections when different species have flowered at the same time. Not only are there interspecific hybrids (*Echeveria* x *Echeveria*), but also there are intergeneric hybrids between *Echeveria* and *Graptopetalum* = *Graptoveria*; *Sedum* = *Sediveria*; *Dudleya* = *Dudleveria*; *Pachyphytum* = *Pachyveria*.

Many of the species of *Echeverias* can be found in garden centres and nurseries. *Echeveria agavoides*, so named because the rosette resembles an agave, is a favourite. The leaves are pointed, but not dangerous, and they are usually plain green. However, if more recently reintroduced material is available the leaves may have a red margin. The plants are often solitary and the rosettes may reach 30 cm (12 in) in diameter. Closely related to this species is *E. purpusorum*. It is smaller headed and not so fast growing, but is has lovely purple flecking to the leaves.

E. elegans is a commonly found bluish-leaved species, which will offset and provide the grower with a constant supply of plants for

Below: ***Echeveria gibbiflora*** **'Carunculata' has characteristic strange protrusions on its upper leaf**

Above: ***Echeveria subrigida*** **is one of the most desirable plants in this genus**

fetes and fairs. A somewhat larger bluish-leaved species is *E. gibbiflora* 'Carunculata'. When the plant is in full growth, a strange protuberance appears on the upper surface of the leaves, not unlike the wattle of a turkey; perhaps it is better described as a series of warts. In winter, when the leaves are not growing so fast, this growth may subside and the leaves return to 'normal'.

E. pulidonis is a favourite yellow-flowered species with blue, red-margined leaves, and the individual heads do not get too large, 9 cm (3½ in) in diameter, but it does clump in time.

Of the heavily farinose species, *E. subridgida*, which can attain the size of a large-headed dudleya, is a desirable plant. It is, however, a little more difficult, for it has a tendency to rot off at ground level and then is not easy to reroot. It usually has a single rosette and does not normally offset, although cutting the centre out may make it shoot, making it possible to obtain some seed and to raise more plants that way.

E. laui, from Mexico, is perhaps the species with the thickest leaves. It also has a white farina over them, and there is a most attractive flower spike, which has large, powdery white bracts protecting the flowers. *E. runyonii*, from Mexico, is another heavily farinose plant. The leaves on this species, in cross-section, are like an inverted V and slightly curved.

A small, crinkly edged leaf species which has bluish-grey to pink leaves is *E. shaviana*. This is not a large-growing species, keeping to a 10 cm (4 in) pot quite happily for some time. This one can be a finicky grower.

Of the hairy species *E. setosa* must be a favourite, sending out hairy flower spikes with yellow and red flowers. This species does clump up, and the offsets may be removed to make more plants and to keep the original to a manageable size. *E. leutotricha* is perhaps the most densely haired species but is perhaps a little more difficult to obtain.

With the exception of *E. leucotricha* and *E. gibbiflora*, the species discussed so far are stemless. Many of the hybrid echeverias will grow quite a tall stem in time. If this becomes too much of a totem pole the remedy is simple: cut the rosette off the stem at a reasonable height, leave it to dry and callous over, for a few days and then pot it up in a sandy soil mixture to root. This is best done at the beginning of the growing season, but can be done as late as late summer, which will give the plant time to establish before winter. Do not throw the stock or bare stem away as this should send out shoots up and down the stem and so give you more progeny.

E. x 'Katella' is one hybrid plant that has become too large in the past and has had the treatment described above. It is now virtually stemless and the best part of 60 cm (2 ft) across. The single head has achieved this size by being regenerated and never having been allowed to flower: every time a flower spike was visible near the centre of the plant and it was big enough, we removed it. In this way all the

Above: *Echeveria* x *'Katella'*

growth went into the plant and not into producing flowers and seed.

On a lot of echeverias it is possible to remove the larger of the flower bracts carefully and set them in sandy soil to root and produce young plants. Taking off the lower leaves from underneath the rosette and setting them in sandy soil may increase your stock of echeverias. Plants gained in these ways will be genetically identical to the parent plants.

There is no doubt that a massed collection of echeverias is a very colourful sight at any time of the year. These plants do need constant attention as they are terribly prone to mealy bug or white woolly aphid. Clear away all the old leaf remains to help control them, and pot on and repot the plants regularly. Only when the plants are moved do all the hiding places for these pests become apparent: they always mass on the side of the plant that is not seen so much. Control of these pests can be biological, by using methylated spirit on a paintbrush, by picking them off with tweezers or your fingers or by using insecticides.

If you use insecticides, then make sure that you read the instructions: do not spray the plants with the mixture as the Crassulaceae are sensitive to the spray and mark easily, especially the heavily adorned species. The best course of action is probably watering the soil with a systemic insecticide during the plants' growing cycle (systemic insecticides are designed to work when the plant is in growth).

Echeverias are not terribly fussy about their growing medium. However, a sandy soil-based compost is the best choice as it is easier to moisten after the winter dry rest and is heavier than a peat-based compost and will therefore act as ballast for any plants that get top-heavy in their pots. It may sometimes be necessary to weight down the pot by putting large pebbles around the top of the pot. To get maximum colour into these attractive plants, they can be stood out of doors for the summer, but the waxy, farinose-leaved plants are better left under protection in case there is a sudden downpour, which will spoil the leaves.

Euphorbia (Euphorbiaceae)

Euphorbias are part of an absolutely enormous family of some 300 genera and 8,000 species. They are to be found almost everywhere in the world and range from highly succulent plants, small weeds, trees, rock plants, herbaceous plants to sea-shore plants.

Their common name is milkweed or spurge, and as the former name suggests the stems contain a milky sap that bleeds or oozes out of the plant if the stems are cut or damaged. Some species of the succulent euphorbias are under extreme pressure when they are in full growth and so the sap can spurt out in any direction. Be careful not to get this milky sap into an open wound, your eyes or any other vulnerable part of your anatomy. Should this happen accidentally, thoroughly wash the affected area with cold, clean water repeatedly and consult your doctor or local hospital emergency centre if swelling occurs. The plant should also be doused in water to stop the sap from leaking. Do not be so alarmed that you will not consider growing these plants. Care is all that is required.

There are at least 1,200 succulent species of euphorbia to choose from for your collection. Both succulent and non-succulent species have the same reproductive parts, and both male and female flowers are needed to complete the process. In some species this means having two plants (at least), and in other species one plant bears both male and female flowers.

Euphorbia pulcherrima is a good and well known plant to use to illustrate the flower structure of these plants. Although you may never have heard of *E. pulcherrima*, you will probably be familiar with it under its common name, poinsettia. Those lovely large red, white or pink 'petals' are, in fact, not petals but rather colourful bracts; the flowers do not have petals. When the seed pod develops it will have three chambers and only three seeds, if they have all developed properly. Flowering, however, does continue throughout the year, given a high enough temperature in the winter.

Probably the next best known euphorbia is the houseplant *E. milii*, the crown of thorns. This is a succulent although it is also quite woody stemmed and drops its leaves if underwatered. This plant is capable of reaching 3.5 m (12 ft) in height and as much across. If it outgrows its welcome as a houseplant, it can easily be pruned to a more manageable size, and the cuttings rooted in a sandy, multi-purpose compost. If kept in sufficient light *E. milii* should flower year round. The usual bract colour is scarlet, but white, yellow and pink or pale red are available. On the original species the bracts are rather small, but more recent hybrids have larger bracts and are more showy. It is possible to raise these from seed.

Above: *Euphorbia obesa*, from southern Africa, is one of the more succulent euphorbias

A visit to the Canary Islands will introduce you to euphorbias growing in their natural environment. Of these, *E. canariensis* grows 2–3 m (6–10 ft) high and the same or more across, each thicket being made up of many four-sided stems. They make good pot plants, but eventually get rather tall. *E. atropurpurea*, *E. balsamifera*, *E. regis-jubae* and *E. aphylla* are also commonly occurring species, but these tend to grow into bushes and do not take well to pot culture. *E. mellifera* is a non-succulent euphorbia, which can be grown outdoors in a sheltered spot in frost-free areas, preferably with its back to something warm like a wall or conservatory glass. Another euphorbia that will be found in the Canaries is *E. tirucalli*, which does not occur naturally but has been introduced to gardens, from which it has escaped.

The more desirable and succulent species tend to come from southern Africa and Madagascar. The most succulent is probably *E. obesa*. It has no spines and no leaves but has a round to cylindrical body, ribbed and highly patterned or chequered. It will not tolerate overwatering and requires full sun and freely draining compost. Male and female plants are needed for seed production.

Similar to *E. obesa* are *E. meloformis* and *E. valida*. The main difference is that these plants produce their flowers on long green stalks, which dry to light brown and remain on the plant after the flower is finished, giving the impression that the plant is horned. They produce offsets with age and make clumps, which *E. obesa* does not.

E. bupleurifolia, *E. horrida* and *E. stellaespina* are three South African species that are firm favourites on the show benches. They all clump up with age, although *E. horrida* makes the largest plant of the three. They are all attractive and rewarding plants to grow.

There are many Madagascan species, most of which require greater than average heat during the winter months. The usual solution is a hot box in the greenhouse or bringing them indoors. Those with a similar habit of growth to *E. milii* but not reaching the same dimensions are *E. leuconeura*, *E. lophogona*, *E. neohumbertii*, *E. viguieri* and *E. hislopii*.

There are smaller, lower-growing species from Madagascar, which include *E. decaryi*, *E. capsaintemariensis* and *E. francoisii*. These all have enlarged rootstocks and need careful cultivation; on the other hand they do not need full sun, for they are quite happy in semi-shade.

One rather charming little bush euphorbia with very thin stems, which reach 30 cm (12 in) in cultivation, is *E. antisyphilitica* from the USA and Mexico. In the wild this makes very large, low bushes, but in cultivation it is fairly slow. It has sweet little pink and white flowers during the summer for quite a long period. This plant is unlikely to outgrow a 15 cm (6 in) pot.

The most commonly occurring plants in garden centres are *E. trigonus* with three-sided stems and small deciduous leaves, often with purple red markings on the stems and eventually forming quite large clumps; *E. mammillaris*, which usually has green stems and persistent, small flower stalks; and the clump-forming *E. ferox* with flower stalks that harden to spines. Other species, such as *E. cooperi*, *E. resinifera* and *E. grandialata*, can be found from time to time, but these are potentially large plants. Also seen sometimes are plants of *E. ingens*. This makes a thick four-sided column and grows eventually into a tree 9–12 m (30–40 ft) tall.

Succulent euphorbias are not really grown for their flowers, but for their body forms, colour, markings and spines. Variegated and cristate forms of some species are available for those who like something different, and variegate plants do add a little more colour to an otherwise rather green group of plants. Only a very few names have been mentioned here; there are many more and there is a specialist group concerned with the growing of these plants. New forms are being discovered all the time, particularly from the Indian continent, and it is likely that there are many yet to be discovered and named from South America.

Below: ***Euphorbia cooperi*** **is one of the larger growing species that is widely available**

Above: ***Faucaria tuberculosa*** **in flower in autumn**

Faucaria (Aizoaceae)

This small group of plants is easy and rewarding to grow. They come from East and South East Cape Province in South Africa. They are clumping, stemless, green-leaved plants, sometimes spotted, usually with a keel to the back of the leaf and usually toothed on the leaf inner margin. These teeth give the plants the appearance of a pair of tiger's jaws, as reflected in the species' common name, tiger jaws. There is often a pink or red tinge to the teeth or keel, although plants must be grown in good light to make this develop. The form of these plants is three or four pairs of leaves stacked alternately on top of one another, sometimes branching.

With one exception the flowers are yellow. The exception is *Faucaria candida*, which has white flowers. The flowers are large – up to 5 cm (2 in) in diameter – often swamping the individual heads. They are autumn–winter flowering; *F. candida*, if it flowers late in the year, can have quite a pinkish tinge to the petals. The cold weather seems to enhance the colour as much as sunlight. These plants should be watered during late spring, summer and autumn, although they will not be harmed if accidentally watered at other times. Repotting can be done whenever the plant seems to need it, either because it has reached the edge of its existing pot or because it is wilting.

Faucarias are prone to red spider mite, so keep a careful watch for this pest: tell-tale signs are a rusty appearance on the newer growth, or a very fine webbing over the centre of the growths. Treatment is a proprietary insecticide from your local garden centre. Propagation of these plants is easy either from seed, as with conophytums, or by cuttings.

Species to look for include *F. tigrina*, *F. felina*, *F. candida and F. tuberculosa*, which, as the name suggest, has warts on the upper surface of the leaves.

Gasteria (Asphodelaceae)

Gasterias come from the coastal areas of South Africa, usually not penetrating more than 200 m (700 ft) inland. There are many names for plants in cultivation, but only 16 distinct species are recognized plus some subspecies.

Gasterias are most accommodating plants, wanting very little in the way of special treatment, except that they do not like being too cold and damp in the winter because this may cause black spots to appear on the leaves; this is not life threatening but it will disfigure the plant until the affected leaves have grown out. Gasterias do need some water in winter, but not too much. Try and boost the heat a little for them to avoid the black spots.

Gasterias get their name from the swollen base or stomach of each flower. The flowers are borne on a simple, occasionally branched, stem, and are usually green at the tip, followed by orange, fading to yellow at the base. These plants are quite happy flowering at almost any time of the year, but the months when the light intensity is best are usually favoured.

Gasterias are not especially fussy about the compost, but it is advisable to include more sand than usual as the fleshy roots of these plants are apt to rot if insufficiently well drained.

Gibbaeum (Aizoaceae)

Gibbaeums are a relatively small group of highly succulent plants that may be found in the South Cape Province and Little Karroo in South Africa. They will mostly be found growing where there are patches or outcrops of quartz and like extremely high light intensity.

The main distinguishing feature of these plants is the unequal length of the two leaves, which are almost united except when plants are in flower or producing a new pair of leaves. In shape, apart from the lack of teeth, they are reminiscent of a shark's jaw.

With a few exceptions, these plants are pubescent (covered with short hairs) to a lesser or greater extent, which acts as protection against the harsh environment and gives them a silvery-white appearance. Most species are low growing, although *Gibbaeum pubescens* and *G. pachypodium* will grow taller in cultivation than they do in the wild. Those species without hairs include *G. petrense*, *G. comptonii*, *G. heathii*, *G. luckhoffii* and *G. gibbosum*. A few species – *G. haagei*, *G. schwantesii* and *G. velutinum* – have much longer leaves and are scarcely united at all.

Many growers find these plants are shy to flower, partly because each has its own set growing time and cannot be made to grow at any different time. In addition, most want to flower in winter in the northern hemisphere, when daylight hours are at their shortest. Count it as an achievement if you do manage to get them to flower. The flower colours are white or, more usually, purple. There is another plant in circulation that looks like *G. velutinum* but it has orange flowers, which is a hybrid with a glottiphyllum.

Propagation is from seed or cuttings.

Greenovia (Crassulaceae)

The *Greenovia* is another charming little succulent genus from the Canary Islands off the west coast of Africa. There are only two or three species, and they are all equally easy to

Above: ***Greenovia dodrantalis*** **from the Canary Islands**

grow. *Greenovia dodrantalis* is perhaps the best species to recommend here because it offsets freely. *G. aurea* tends to remain solitary, which can be disastrous should the only head decide to flower, because it is a monocarpic species.

These ground-hugging, blue-grey, glaucous-leaved plants are winter growing. During the summer months, when they are resting, the rosettes of leaves close up, looking for all the world like a blue rose bud. In autumn, with moister, cooler weather, the 'buds' begin opening up. Flowering, when it does occur, is at the end of the winter or in early spring. We have never found seedlings appearing spontaneously from these plants and must therefore deduce that they are self-sterile.

We have recently planted some three or four plants out of doors on a rockery in a sheltered position; although they have had some frosts, so far they are alive and thriving. The test will come if snow lies on the crowns of the plants. As a safeguard, give some protection in the form of horticultural fleece, bracken or a pane of glass.

Haworthia (Asphodelaceae)

Haworthia, a genus of approximately 70 species, originates in southern Africa. This genus tends to grow in the winter in the northern hemisphere. The species are generally low growing, rosette forming and clumping. Leaf shape ranges from truncate and windowed to almost grass-like. Add a handful of sharp sand or grit to the growing compost because these plants often have enlarged, fleshy roots that will rot in poorly draining conditions. The haworthias are free-flowering plants, although their flowers are not very exciting. They are borne on a thin stem 10–30 cm (4–12 in) tall and are mostly white-cream with perhaps a hint of pink. They hybridize among themselves, and some interesting offspring have developed on occasion. Generally though, hybridizing these little succulents only causes more confusion.

Haworthia attenuata f. *clariperla* is one of the most attractively marked species and quite easy to grow. It offsets well and can therefore be given to admiring friends. The horizontal

Below: ***Haworthia minima*** **is a delightful clump-forming species with thick leaves**

white lines on the back of the dark green leaves are usually quite well raised.

H. minima is a delightfully marked species, clump forming with thick leaves, which have more or less pronounced white tubercles. It is not very fast growing and worth keeping the clumps intact. Remember, it is always prudent to remove one offset and pot it up to keep as a reserve in case the main plant dies.

The cultivar *H. venosa* 'Coriacea' is a very large-leaved form of what is sometimes still called *H. tesselata*. This whole group of haworthias is very well-marked with square or tesselate patterns on the leaf surfaces. The Coriacea is a very good species with which to begin a collection.

There are many retuse species of haworthia, and they are a delight to behold. These highly windowed varieties take on an exceedingly glossy appearance when they are fully turgid and a somewhat more mat-like appearance when they are resting. A few species to look out for are *H. comptoniana*, *H. retusa* (and varieties) and, perhaps the best of all, *H. emelyae*.

Above: One of the most attractively marked haworthias, *H. attenuata* f. *clariperla*

Hoya (Asclepiadaceae)

The common name for hoyas is wax flower. The 90 or so species range from Indonesia and the surrounding area to the Himalayas. Often they are epiphytic and are twining or vining plants. They are highly attractive to mealy bug aphids, for the plants exude large amounts of nectar from their flowers and leaf axils. Some species have very tough, persistent leaves, while others have smaller, thinner leaves that are shed if the conditions are too sunny or too dry. Many can grow to whatever size you want. Most species bear colourful and sweetly scented flowers.

In the wild hoyas are accustomed to protection from much larger plants or trees and therefore often live in semi-shade. For this reason they make very good houseplants. The most commonly grown species is *Hoya carnosa*, but it does not live up to the common name, because the individual flowers – and there may be 20 to 30 in each individual umbel

Above: ***Huernia primulina***

or bunch – are not waxy but are quite felted with glass-like, raised coronas. With all of the hoyas it is important that, once they have flowered, the flowering peduncle is not removed because the plants will continue to flower from the same peduncle. *H. carnosa* comes in variegated forms and there is even a form with deformed leaves. Often the two characteristics are combined.

H. bella is also available as a houseplant and makes a good hanging-basket subject. However, it really does not like being in the sun. This little hoya has glassy flowers, which don't look real. It is a delightfully perfumed species.

H. multiflora is another popular species. It is sometimes given the common name shooting rocket because the flowers have reflexed petals, which make them look as if they are little rockets.

H. cinnamomifolia looks remarkably like *H. carnosa* until it flowers. It has fewer flowers in the umbel, the petals are backward pointing and the coronas are a dark cinnamon colour.

It is doubtful if any of the hoyas can truly be considered as succulent, but they are very close relatives of many similar plants and so creep in by association. If plants such as *H. carnosa* are considered succulent, then *Stephanotis floribunda* should also be included.

Propagation can be from seed but is more usually from cuttings.

Huernia (Asclepiadaceae)

The huernias are among the easiest of the stapeliads to grow, and they do not have unpleasant-smelling flowers. Most species are quite small but very free flowering. *Huernia namaquensis* var. *hallii* has pretty spotted flowers about 2.5 cm (1 in) in diameter. *H. primulina* has larger yellow flowers, and *H. boleana* has bigger stems and larger flowers with extended, lobed petals.

Jatropha (Euphorbiaceae)

This large group of plants, which are closely related to euphorbias, are widespread throughout the tropics. Many species are available as they grow readily from seed, but, as with *Euphorbia*, the genus contains herbaceous and evergreen shrubs as well as succulents. All parts contain a milky sap, which may irritate the skin, and some herbaceous plants have leaves with barbed hairs.

Jatropha podagrica is grown in continental Europe as a houseplant. It has scarlet flowers, both male and female flowers on the same stem. J. *cathartica* (syn. *J. berlandieri*), the most succulent of them all, has a large underground, swollen stem and requires well-drained compost and careful watering.

Below: ***Huernia namaquensis*** **var.** ***hallii***

Above: The oak-leaf form of *Kalanchoe beharensis*

Kalanchoe (Crassulaceae)

Kalanchoe is a very large genus of plants containing over 200 species. They come from Madagascar, southern Africa and extend into Arabia, beyond into India and further east.

Many species have become popular with enthusiasts, particularly those that are easy to propagate. Most available species will grow in the summer months, although flowering often takes place in winter.

The most frequently sold species is probably *Kalanchoe blossfeldiana*. It is widely available in florists' shops, chain stores, garden centres and hardware stores. This plant comes in a variety of flower colours, from deep red to lemon yellow. The leaves are glossy green with notched edges. You must keep this plant in reasonably good light even when it is not in flower, otherwise it will not repeat its colourful display another year.

K. tubiflora, also known as and recently reinstated as *Bryophyllum tubiflorum*, must be the world's most easily propagated plant. Every narrow leaf on this Madagascan plant is capable of producing, on average, eight new plants, which will be identical to the parent plant. They develop as adventitious plantlets from around the leaf ends, sending roots out into the moist air, and when the leaf begins to wither, these plantlets fall to the ground or the top of the pot in which the parent is growing, and the roots then search for better nourishment by rooting down into the compost. The only way to rid your collection of this plant is to leave it outside for the winter to become frozen. There are around 30 species in the group that behave in this way, but most of them are not in general cultivation. However, *K. diagremontanum* (deltoid-shaped leaves) and *K. rauhii* (leaf shape is between the other two) are species that might be encountered.

K. tomentosa is another very popular species. Its leaves are covered in white hairs with brown hairs at the tips. It forms a multi-stemmed plant and has to reach a height of 45 cm (18 in) to 60 cm (2 ft) before it will flower in the winter to early spring. The flowers are really not that spectacular, being a rather washed out creamy-brown. The beauty of this plant definitely lies in its foliage.

K. beharensis comes from southern Madagascar and will eventually become a tree. The leaves, which are densely covered with short hairs, are slightly serrated and deltoid in shape. When this plant is beyond the seedling or cutting stage and is being watered and fed frequently, the leaves can get quite large: 10–30 cm (4–12 in) long and 20 cm (8 in) broad. They are very tactile, harmless and usually unharmed by being touched. In full sun these leaves take on a bronzed appearance on the upper surface. The new growth lacks this colour being rather white-green, but as soon as the leaves have fully grown they quickly develop their tanned appearance.

Several forms of this plant are available. A heavily lobed variety known as the oak-leaf form; a particularly dark-leaved variety, sometimes sold as 'Chocolate'; a cultivar called 'Fangs', which is hairy to the same degree but in addition has many warty excrescences on the underside of the leaves; and, if you do not like hairy plants, there is even a glaucous or nude form.

It is important to keep potting on these plants. Sideshoots of large specimens can be easily potted on to form new plants. Winter temperature is not too critical, although it will probably do best if kept to a minimum of 7°C (45°F) or a little higher.

K. rhombopilosa is a delightful little kalanchoe with grey chocolate-flecked leaves. The leaves are not terribly well attached to the stem, and if handled at all roughly the plant tends to shed many of its leaves. However, all the leaves will root readily. It does not like winter cold and will need water to stop too many leaves dropping.

Some kalanchoes make excellent hanging-basket subjects. *K. pumila*, from central Madagascar, is primarily a winter grower and will flower in early spring, often putting on an excellent display at Easter. The plant is about 15 cm (6 in) tall, consisting of many shoots that arise from soil level. It has small, crenate, mealy-white leaves, which make a marvellous background for the pink flowers. Some water during the winter months is needed for this plant to flourish.

Below: Various leaf shapes and colours of *Kalanchoe beharensis*

One more kalanchoe to recommend is *K. thyrsiflora*. This plant comes from the Orange Free State, Natal and Transvaal in South Africa. It is predominantly winter growing and flowers in early spring. This plant does branch with age or flowering, but does not grow to more than 30 cm (12 in). The leaves, under greenhouse protection, are about 10 cm (4 in) in diameter and are almost round, but are very thin in cross-section. The white meal covering their surface is easily wiped off. In the wild this mealy appearance is rarely present, and the leaves look quite sunburned, for the elements soon remove the coating. The flowers are worth waiting for, although they are fairly small and lemon-yellow; the perfume is strong and exactly like lily-of-the-valley and any conservatory or greenhouse will be swamped with the scent. Unfortunately, the plant usually dies after flowering, and propagation must be from seed, but sometimes the head that has flowered will produce a number of shoots, so these can be taken off and rooted. Do not overwater this plant.

Lampranthus (Aizoaceae)

These easy-to-grow plants will enjoy being bedded out for the summer and may be left out for the winter. However, take a couple of cuttings and put them under protection as a precaution against a bad winter.

These subshrubs can be erect, spreading or prostrate and have many leaves. Flower colour can be white, pink, red, purple, rose, orange or yellow. To see a bush of *Lampranthus aureus*, with its bright orange flowers in full bloom is truely dazzling. All the species flower well if given half a chance.

Propagation is from seed or cuttings.

Lithops (Aizoaceae)

These plants, known as living stones, are firm favourites with new and established collectors alike. They come from southern Africa, from dry regions with strong light intensity, and it can be difficult for amateurs to provide the conditions they prefer in the wild.

Each head of these stemless, highly succulent plants consists of a single pair of very fat leaves, which are referred to as the head. The upper surface of what might once have been a flat, thin leaf, has been forced to face its opposite leaf because the underside of the flat leaf has become swollen with water-storing cells. The end of the flat leaf has been truncated to form a window through which light is allowed to stream in order that the plant may photosynthesize.

Every year each head – and a plant may have more than one – produces a new pair of leaves, occasionally two pairs of leaves, from the centre or between the two leaves. While these new bodies or heads are emerging and growing, the plants must be allowed to rest and must not be watered. Once the new bodies have fully emerged and the old leaves have become papery thin or leathery, recommence watering. It is important that these plants are never left standing in water; always let the surplus water drain right away.

Lithops prefer a loam-based compost with added sand or grit, and very good drainage is essential. Repotting is best carried out at the beginning of their growing season, which is late spring or early summer in the northern hemisphere. Do not give them a rich compost to grow in; if they are repotted or potted on every three to four years, it should not be necessary to feed them. It is easy to overfeed these highly succulent plants, but this weakens the epidermis, stretches it and can cause the heads to rot off. Little can be done when this occurs; with a multi-headed plant it may be possible to salvage one or two heads, but more often than not the fungus will have infected all the heads.

Above: ***Lithops bella*****, a white-flowered species, flowers in the autumn**

It is almost essential to have a greenhouse in which to grow these plants. However, we have seen some very well-grown specimens in an apartment. The owner had a balcony and was able to put the plants outside for the summer without fear of them getting too wet or slugs and snails attacking them. The plants were brought in before the weather became too cold and were put on a table in front of the window. Trying to grow these plants on a windowsill is not easy because many houses have double-glazed windows that cut down considerably on the amount of useful light. A single-glazed window should be satisfactory, if it is south or west facing.

Lithops do not like hot humid conditions: they need cool nights in order to grow and flower well. Coolness also intensifies the leaf colours. It is not unknown for these plants to receive frost and snow in the wild, although it is not recommended that this particular weather condition be emulated in cultivation. In winter the plants really do not need to be kept particularly warm, 5°C (40°F) is all that is required. When they are growing during the late spring, summer and autumn it is important to let them have plenty of air passing over their heads. Stagnant, hot air is lethal to these plants, as the bodies will boil and you will be

Above: ***Lithops aucampiae*****, a yellow-flowered 'stone plant'**

left with a mushy shell of a plant. To provide good air circulation in a greenhouse it may be necessary to install two small fans. It is far better to increase air movement than it is to put up shading over the greenhouse glass.

It is a pity that, when these charming little plants are offered for sale in garden centres, they are often displayed in a heavily shaded area. This only makes the plants 'soft' and likely to rot, so it really is not in the best interests of garden centres.

The flowers on lithops are white, yellow or yellow with a white centre, and they are produced towards the autumn. Some forms of *Lithops pseudotruncatella* may flower as early in the year as early summer in some temperate areas, but the white-flowered species usually flower later in the year.

Yellow-flowered species recommended for growing are *L. pseudotruncatella*, *L. aucampiae*, *L. hookeri* and *L. lesliei*. Recommended white-flowering species include *L. salicola* and *L. karasmontana*. Some cultivars are available with body colours different from the usual species; for example, *L. optica* has a greyish-green body but *L. optica* var. *rubra* has ruby red leaves. This phenomenon does make the cultivars more difficult to grow, so initially it might be better to ignore these and to settle for growing the more normal forms.

Lithops are easily raised from seed as long as the seed is not covered or put in a dark place, because the Aizoaceae family needs light in order to stimulate germination. The seed-dispersal mechanism for many of this family is ingenious. The seed capsules develop after the plants have flowered and dry to a hard bud. When the rains come this bud or capsule absorbs the moisture and opens up the 'petals', more accurately valves, and the capsule looks for all the world like a flower opening. The seeds are then splashed out by the rain drops and fall to the ground. If the rain is not persistent, the capsule will close up and wait for more rain before opening again, when the conditions for germination of the seed should be better. The botanical term for this is hygrochastic.

Nolina (Nolinaceae)

This genus of succulent plants originates mainly in Mexico. The species most often found in garden centres is *Nolina recurvata*, the pony tail palm. They make very good house plants and can stand outside for the summer months. The plants on sale have often had their centres deliberately removed or damaged to force them to produce many growing points or shoots, which occurs naturally with age but only after flowering. It has to be quite large to flower, say 1–1.2 m (3–4 ft) in height. Like the agaves, these plants need to be potted on regularly to attain a statuesque size.

Pachyphytum (Crassulaceae)

Closely related to echeveria, pachyphytums come solely from Mexico. There are some 12 species, and each of these is clump forming. They hybridize readily with echeverias, and there may be a hybrid with a sedum.

The leaves of the rosettes are often quite tightly compacted, so much so that they impress their outline on the preceding and following leaves. The other genus of succulent

Above: ***Nolina recurvata*, the pony tail palm, is a good patio plant for frost-free environments**

plant in which this is encountered is *Agave*. The leaves on most of the species are bluish with a dusting of farina in some species.

The plants flower freely, bearing long, curved flower spikes, which have bell-shaped flowers, usually red or dusky pink, with large bracts encasing the individual flowers. There is usually a copious amount of nectar, which can drip on other plants should they be nearby.

The species that are usually available are *Pachyphytum hookeri*, which is small leaved and compact growing, and *P. glutinicaule*, with a sticky stem. *P. oviferum*, commonly known as sugared almond plant, can range from quite a large mass of heads to a container 60 cm (2 ft) across, but this takes some careful growing as the leaves are marked easily and potting on is difficult without doing damage to the plant.

P. viride is a very robust, green-leaved species with greenish-white petals to the flowers and red inner parts. It is not that fast growing, but it will grow a little taller than some of the species, to about 30 cm (12 in).

Pachypodium (Apocynaceae)

This genus of succulent plants contains about 13 species, which come from southern Africa and Madagascar. All require well-drained compost and no overwatering. Coming in various shapes and sizes, all of the plants have spines or thorns.

The two easiest and very similar species to grow are *Pachypodium lamerei*, with green shiny leaves, and *P. geayi*, with darker, narrower leaves. They are very suitable for indoor culture and can reach a height of 8 m (26 ft) in the wild, but a third of that height is more realistic under glass. *P. lamerei* will flower at a height of 2 m (6 ft) bearing white, scented flowers at its crown. Similar to these two species, but from Namibia rather than from Madagascar, is *P. namaquanum*, which is also known by its common name, half mans. This plant is much slower in growth and really does need a sunny spot in a greenhouse or conservatory.

Other species that require a little more care in their cultivation are *P. baronii* with light red flowers; *P. baronii* 'Windsori' with bright red flowers; *P. densiflorum* with its dark yellow flowers; *P. rosulatum*, with light yellow flowers; and *P. brevicaule* with its chrome yellow flowers. Propagation for all of these plants is from seed.

Below: Pachyphytums are attractive and easily grown succulents

Pedilanthus (Euphorbiaceae)

The last genus in this large family that is worth mentioning is one that occurs in the garden centre trade from time to time. Usually it is not displayed with the other cacti and succulents, but is placed with the houseplants, which gives us a clue as to the best conditions in which to grow it. The pedilanthus come entirely from the Americas, and are known to occur mostly in Mexico, although it may simply be a question of other species not having been discovered and named.

Pedilanthus tithymaloides is the plant that is most often found offered for sale, and when it is, it is usually in its variegated form. It is a many-stemmed plant, jointed to the point of zigzagging, with green, variegated leaves for about half its height. If it decides to flower, and this particular species seems somewhat shy, the flowers will be red, to many people resembling a red bird.

P. macrocarpus is jointed, but the joints stay more or less in a straight line, reaching a height of 2 m (6 ft) without any trouble at all. It needs to be potted on regularly to keep it growing well and flowering. The flowers are red and like small birds. This particular species has very felted stems, which gives the stems a grey appearance, and very tiny, ephemeral leaves. This plant will often produce monstrose growths, possibly because of accelerated growth. Given a free root run, this montrose growth is even more abundant, although the flowering is less.

Propagation of these plants is from seed (three seeds to a pod) or from cuttings. Cuttings seem to take a long time to get going – often one to two years. It is worth tying

Above: ***Pleiospilos nelii*****'s natural habitat is the granite rocks of the southern part of South Africa**

several thin stems together with raffia and planting the bundle.

Piaranthus (Asclepiadaceae)

The piaranthus have a similar growth pattern to the duvalias and are also easy to grow, but the flowers are lighter in colour than the duvalias and spotted. They have an unpleasant smell.

Pleiospilos (Aizoaceae)

These chunky, granite-like, highly succulent plants come from the tablelands of the Little and Great Karroos and Cape Province in South Africa. They are a dark bluish-grey in colour, finely and densely spotted, with a burnished red appearance if they are grown in full sun. They are easy plants to keep and fairly undemanding. With some species a pair of leaves can reach a combined length of 18–20 cm (7–8 in), although their width is not usually this great.

In the wild the plants are successful because of their strong resemblance to their surroundings: the granitic rocks. In all probability the plants were a lot more diverse eons ago, but it is those that most closely resembled their surroundings that survived and produced further plants like themselves.

The chunkiest of these plants, *Pleiospilos bolusii, P. simulans* and *P. nelii*, normally have one pair of leaves, although, like the lithops, they produce a new pair of leaves each year and the old pair is absorbed; so for a period there may be two sets of leaves stacked one on the other and at right angles. *P. compactus* and its forms can have up to four pairs of leaves, usually less chunky and longer.

These plants grow in the latter half of the year in the northern hemisphere, so it is best to commence watering in midsummer, as long as the majority of the old leaves have dried up and have become very leathery. Flower buds will appear in late midsummer and may be from one to five in number, coming from between the newest leaf pair, with the oldest bud in the centre and the others either side in a line. The flowers are quite large, getting bigger with each day that they are open. They are golden-yellow in colour with an orange tinge to the outermost petals. The petals eventually fade to a reddish-orange and flop over the leaves, so try to get them off the leaves by twisting them out of the way. After flowering, which can continue into late autumn, the plants begin to push through new leaves from the same point as the flowers. At least one new head should appear, and if conditions have been good perhaps two heads will appear and, as a result, the plant will increase its size.

One species, *P. nelii*, does not normally flower until late winter depending on the weather. The flowers actually come from the new heads – that is, the plant produces the new body before budding up. This species also has much more rounded leaves than the others. The flower is a salmon-orange, but because of the lateness of the flower there is always the danger that it will not develop fully. Propagation of these plants is usually from seed, but they will root from cuttings if necessary.

Sansevieria (Dracaenaceae)

This extensive genus which is found in Africa, Madagascar, India and Indonesia, has one representative which must be in thousands of homes throughout the world and the owners probably do not even know they have a succulent: *Sansevieria trifasciata* or mother-in-law's tongue! It can outgrow a 38 cm (15 in) pot quite quickly and can be divided regularly. This particular species comes in a variety of guises, the most boring is the plain, dark green-leaved form. The variegated forms are far more interesting, having either a yellow stripe down each edge of the leaf or a yellow stripe through the middle. The leaves usually have horizontal banding. These plants sometimes produce flowers, although the flower spikes on these particular species are not huge. The flowers open in the evening and can be quite highly scented, like hyacinth perfume. A more easily housed cultivar is *S. trifasciata* 'Golden Hahnii', which has much shorter rosettes and proliferates more slowly.

Some species, including *S. pinguicula*, have a habit of 'walking' across the ground or on top of a pot, with their new offsets. They produce a stolon above ground and the plantlet on the end then puts down roots when it is a short distance from its parent. Some species, such as *S. cylindrica* with cylindrical stems, can be quite slow growing. *S. grandis* is perhaps the largest species, producing a flower spike up to 1.2 m (4 ft) tall. *S. aethiopica* is a small species that does very well in cultivation, offsetting and flowering easily, and it also has a quite large flower spike, again highly perfumed. All in all, this genus is a very long-suffering one and will tolerate most conditions.

Sedum (Crassulaceae)

There is a large number of species, commonly called stonecrops, in this genus and they are very widespread throughout the world. The 400 or so species come from very varied habitats in Japan, China, Mongolia, Siberia, North America, Mexico, Peru, Morocco and Europe. There are species suitable for rockeries, herbaceous borders, hanging baskets and containers in greenhouses.

Some of the common hardy species suitable for the rockery are *Sedum kamtschaticum*, coming in plain or variegated leaf form with golden flowers; *S. spathulifolium*, a small-rosetted, white-leaved plant, whose older leaves, denuded of their farina, are a purple colour; *S. populifolium*, which dies down in winter; *S. spurium*, an exceedingly common pink-flowered plant; the yellow-flowered *S. rosea* of which the herbaceous parts die down to a gnarled rootstock each winter.

S. spectabile is an absolute must for any garden with its umbels of pink flowers that are highly attractive to the last of the butterflies and bees of the year. Similar to *S. spectabile* is *S.* 'HerbstFreude', but with less showy reddish flowers. These plants are not generally accepted as succulent species.

Among the species recommended for hanging baskets under glass during winter, possibly to be moved outside for the summer, is *S. morganianum*, which is sometimes called the burro's tail sedum. It makes dense masses of hanging stems to 30 cm (12 in) long. Good light is essential, otherwise the leaves will become even more loosely attached than they are usually. The one failing with this species is that the leaves are easily knocked off the stems. Every leaf that falls will send out roots and a new plant will form, but a bare stem is the result. Red flowers appear at the ends of the trailing stems. There is another similar but not quite so common species, *S. burrito*, which has smaller and more rounded leaves that are not shed so readily.

S. sieboldii must be the sedum most frequently sold in shops and garden centres. It is

Above: *Sedum lucidum*, although not hardy, is commonly found in one of its colour forms, which range from green to red to variegated

extremely accommodating, and the colour of the leaves is enhanced if it is grown in sunlight. Either out of doors or in a porch or conservatory, the stems reach about 30 cm (12 in) long; the leaves are small, almost round and flattened, glaucous, with varying amounts of red and pink in them according to the amount of light received. If this plant is grown out of doors permanently, the stems will be shorter. The flowers are pink and appear in the autumn. Equally common is the variegated form, which is perhaps a little shyer.

S. treleasei is an extremely common succulent plant from Mexico. The upright, unbranched stems attain a height of nearly 60 cm (2 ft), which means that there is a danger that, if it is not given enough good-quality light, the stems will fall over or even break off under their own weight. The usual form is quite glaucous, but a more pruinose form, 'Haren', is available. The flowers are borne on a flat-topped inflorescence.

S. lucidum is another commonly grown plant, although it is possible that it is masquerading under the name of *S.* x *rubrotinctum*, perhaps even more common. *S. lucidum* is identical in habit but with smaller leaves and does not get so tall.

Of the more desirable species, or more commonly exhibited sedums, *S. suaveolens* is a good example. This particular species is very similar in appearance to *Echeveria subridgida* or one of the large-headed dudleyas. Indeed, when it is not bearing evidence of its flowers it is often mistaken for the former. The plant is stemless and often solitary, although it will clump with age, the individual heads reaching 23 cm (9 in) across before sending out stolons. The leaves are glaucous, and the flower stems emerge from fairly low down on the plant and are initially indistinguishable from the stolons; the flowers are white with dark red anthers.

S. hintonii is chiefly winter growing and flowering. It is a small-growing plant with densely white, bristly-haired, blue leaves and dies down after flowering. Because this is an autumn–winter grower, it is important to give it very little water during the worst months of the year, and on no account to get any water on the leaves, which will rot. It is always worth growing those plants that are susceptible to overwatering in clay pots so that the compost dries out more quickly.

S. greggii is another widely grown, small species although it is often seen unnamed. This plant dies down in the resting period after flowering in midsummer. New growth from the bases of the old flowering stems is cone-like and pale green. These new heads also occur along the length of the old flower stem and can easily be removed for propagation.

S. craigii, with its bluish-pink leaves, has become more popular and will make a suitable subject for a hanging basket in the greenhouse. It too has white flowers. *S. furfuraceum* has become widespread in collections. Its leaves are small, dark green fading to red as the leaves mature; it has white flowers and is easily cultivated from cuttings.

S. palmeri is worth trying on a rockery when you have enough plant material. It has thin, blue, glaucous, round leaves and forms clumps of stems. The yellow flowers are borne on an arched inflorescence near the top of the stem.

Some sedums reach such large proportions that they are referred to as tree sedums. *S. frutescens* is perhaps the best known and most often grown species, which can reach 90 cm (3 ft) at least in height. It really does have a trunk with papery bark, which is always in a state of peeling. This tan-coloured bark is thick enough to write on with a ball-point pen, should the mood take you. The young stems are very brittle and will not stand being moved suddenly or knocked. They do become tougher with age however, and pieces that are accidentally broken off root easily but do take a little time to take on their characteristic tree-like appearance.

Many worthwhile species have been omitted here through lack of space, but do look around your garden centres and nurseries for hardy species and also for some different species to try under cover.

Sempervivum (Crassulaceae)

These hardy succulents occur naturally in alpine regions of North Africa and Europe. Ideally suited to rockeries, they can be too well treated if grown in pots, but do not be put off from doing so. Whatever the situation they are being grown in, rock garden or succulent greenhouse, they need a very well-drained, soil-based compost with added horticultural grit. They also benefit from a topdressing of small grit or fine gravel, to keep the leaves above any damp conditions. Slugs and snails adore these juicy plants but are somewhat selective, preferring the slower growing, choicest plants.

With all sempervivums, the individual heads die after each one has flowered. Hopefully, long before they flower the plants will have produced many offsets. Occasionally, however, a plant may flower before reproducing vegetatively and unless seed is forthcoming that will be the end of the plant. If you have several sempervivums, and two plants flower at the same time, there is a danger that they will hybridize. Sempervivums have been collected extensively. Because they propagate easily from offsets and root in days, it is not

Below: ***Sempervivum ciliosum*** **var.** ***borisii*** **is a rather choice form that has recently become popular**

surprising that the specimens that were first collected were passed around rapidly. It is not unusual to find whole collections of these delightful little rosettes growing in pots on garage roofs. Indeed, sempervivums can often be found growing on roofs themselves, getting a tenacious toe-hold on life with their fine hair-like roots; they almost look like moss growing on the tiles.

Sempervivum rosettes range in size from 5 mm to15 cm (⅛–6 in) in diameter; in leaf colour they range from pale to deep green to blue to deep mahogany red. Flower colour may be white, yellow, rose or red. The best-known species must be the cobweb houseleek, *Sempervivum arachnoideum*. It has a fine white webbing stretching from leaf tip to leaf tip; the individual rosettes are variable in size depending on the form being grown, but typically they are only 2.5 cm (1 in) in diameter. Some of the varieties have a very good colouring to their leaves, becoming quite reddened in the height of summer.

A rather choice sempervivum is *S. ciliosum* var. *borisii*. This is similar to *S. arachnoideum*, but it does have larger heads, up to 6.5 cm (2¼ in). This species does not like too much moisture during the winter months; it will become very gross, open and lax if not kept dry. It does not require a heated greenhouse but will need protection from the winter moisture that occurs in most temperate areas. A clay pan is an essential for this plant.

There are about 40 species of sempervivum, but countless hybrids and cultivars. Some other genera tend, wrongly, to be lumped in with sempervivum, including *Jovibarba*, *Rosularia* and *Sempervivella*.

Senecio (Asteraceae)

These succulents are closely related to the weed groundsel. The inflorescences are composed of many small flowers, which scarcely have petals, just stamens and anthers, and they have the same seed-dispersal mechanism as groundsel: the tufts of silk with a seed attached at the end, which is borne off by the wind to germinate a fair distance from its parent and so not compete with its parent for moisture and nutrients.

There are more than 1,000 species in the genus, of which only about 100 are in cultivation. They come from central and southern Africa, Madagascar, the Canary Islands, Arabia and Mexico to name the prime areas, although there are some species in other countries of the world. Most of the species are easy to cultivate and are often favoured by beginners to the hobby. However, as with other genera, the species that come from Madagascar need extra warmth in winter.

The most commonly available species include *Senecio articulatus*, the candle plant. It is happy growing in almost any conditions, but if plants have too much food and water they will grow very tall or long, for they tend naturally to clamber rather than to keep upright. The new growth has lobed, glaucous leaves, which it sheds when resting. The flowers are cream coloured and, like many senecios, not very pleasant smelling. *S. rowleyanus*, the string of beads plant, makes a good hanging-basket subject and will root from almost every leaf pair internode. It rarely flowers in captivity but it is not grown for the flower. *S. amaniensis* from Tanzania has large, round, flat white leaves. It can grow to a height of 60 cm (2 ft), although length might be more appropriate because this plant tends to get quite top heavy and is reluctant to stand up without support. The terminal inflorescence produced in late summer to autumn has orange flowers and smells atrocious. Cultivation is easy from the shoots that appear in the leaf axils after the plant has flowered. Occasionally shoots appear from the base.

S. kleinia is a tree senecio from the Canary Islands, which can grow up to 3 m (10 ft). It grows during the autumn and winter, flowering at the beginning of its growing period.

Another tree senecio from Mexico is *S. praecox*. This has large palmate leaves and reaches a similar height to *S. kleinia*. The flowers on *S. praecox* are golden-yellow. Some people claim that they have an unpleasant smell. In cultivation this plant is prone to red spider mite and needs to be treated regularly and probably placed out of doors for the summer.

S. stapeliiformis is a very popular species, partly because it is easily propagated but also because it has distinctive purple-red stripes up the stem. The flowers are a good strong scarlet colour. *S. picticaulis* from Kenya, Tanzania, Sudan and Ethiopia has a similar growth form to *S. articulatus*, perhaps not quite so jointed, but with candy-floss pink flowers, and for that reason is worth including in your collection.

Some senecios develop underground tubers, and of this group *S. fulgens* and *S. nyikensis* are the most common species. Both species have glaucous evergreen leaves, and bright red flowers. Finally, a hairy-leaved or woolly-leaved senecio, *S. haworthii*, also sometimes available under the name *Kleinia tomentosa* must be mentioned. In cultivation this plant should be upright, but given the less than perfect light conditions that most of us have during the winter months, it tends to get rather lax. Although it is rare to see this plant in flower in cultivation when it does flower the flowers should be yellow.

Stomatium (Aizoaceae)

Stomatiums come from South Africa, the Orange Free State and Cape Province in particular. They are related to *Faucaria* but are generally smaller and have nocturnal flowers, whereas *Faucaria* are day-flowering species.

Above: ***Senecio nyikensis*** **is one of the more common species. It has impressive bright red flowers**

These plants can be yellow or white flowered. Interestingly, the two flower colour groups must attract different pollinators because their perfumes are quite different; the yellow flowers are quite citrusy, whereas the white flowers remind one of bananas.

They grow in the open, perhaps up against a rock, but they do get very baked. However, cultivation is easy. They are not at all finicky in their requirements, but a fairly well-drained compost is advisable, if they are not to become too lax. Each plant consists of a number of small rosettes of paired, alternate leaves. The leaf edges have white raised tubercles or warts, and the white-flowered species tend to have a greyer appearance than the yellow-flowered species, the leaves of which are a much brighter green.

Recommended yellow-flowering species are *Stomatium agninum* (no tubercles), *S. geoffreyi*, *S. integrum* (no tubercles), *S. jamesii*, *S. loganii* and *S. pyrodorum* (which smells of pears).

Recommended white-flowered species are *S. alboroseum*, *S. meyeri* and *S. niveum*. Often these white flowers have a degree of pink in the petal tips, which is brought out by the cold as these plants usually flower in the late autumn, but may also flower in the early spring. Cultivation is usually from seed, but cuttings may be taken.

Titanopsis (Aizoaceae)

These little plants come from southern Namibia and from West and Central Cape Province in South Africa. This small group of plants is highly adapted to its surroundings and conditions. They are not easy to grow in cultivation, requiring very well-drained compost with added limestone. More success may be had if the plants are grown in clay or terracotta pots rather than in plastic ones, to encourage the soil to dry out more quickly between waterings. Other points to remember are that maximum light conditions are needed for these little treasures, and do not overpot them.

The species available are *Titanopsis calcarea*, *T. fulleri*, *T. hugo-schlecteri*, *T. primosii* and *T. schwantesii*. They have warty leaves to a lesser or greater extent, and these warts may be on the edge of the leaf, or randomly spaced on the face of the leaves. The plants are made up of several rosettes of alternating leaf pairs and branch in time. Leaf colour is often bluish tinged with pink, and the warts may be white. The roots are often thickened, requiring better than average drainage. The afternoon-opening flowers are mostly yellow, although *T. hugo-schlecteri*, whose leaves are almost a reddish-brown, has pinkish-orange flowers. *T. hugo-schlecteri* is also the most difficult species to keep. The growing period is from late summer to midwinter in the northern hemisphere, although if the atmosphere is particularly damp then it may be prudent to withhold watering until the humidity decreases.

Propagation is from seed, and the plants are unlikely to outgrow a 12.5 cm (5 in) pot.

Below: ***Titanopsis calcarea*** **is one of the readily available plants of this genus**

Trichodiadema (Aizoaceae)

The genus *Trichodiadema* is excellent for beginners. Unfortunately, people who have been growing them for some time often neglect these plants, possibly because they are so common. This group of some 30 species is from a fairly widespread area, ranging from southern Namibia, West and South Cape Province to one or two little pockets of plants in the Orange Free State in South Africa. These smallish plants have leaf tips that bear a cluster of dark brown, more or less spreading bristles, the diadem from which part of the plant name comes (*tricho* means hair).

The most rewarding species to grow must be *Trichodiadema bulbosum*. It has a tuberous rootstock, which can be exposed above soil level in a pot or a bonsai container. If the topgrowth gets too lax or rampant the shears can be taken to it, but bear in mind that the purple flowers are borne on the new growth, so choose the time carefully to give the plant a trim.

T. densum is a plant that we acquired quite early in our collecting careers and had to reacquire more recently. It makes a dense mound of short green leaves with the diadems at the leaf tips almost touching each other. This is a very good species for flowering.

T. stellatum is low growing and mat forming, producing masses of pale purple flowers in late autumn. It almost looks dead when it is not growing, but a good soaking towards the end of summer will revitalize the plant in time for it to flower on time.

Not all trichodiademas have purple or pink flowers; some species, *T. mirabile* for example, have white flowers.

Propagation is from seed or cuttings, except for those that have annual growth.

There is a specialist international group that promotes the entire Aizoaceae family, and more information can be obtained by contacting it. Contact details can be found on the Internet.

Tylecodon (Crassulaceae)

Until 1978 this genus of succulent plants was included in the genus *Cotyledon*. It does not take a crossword expert to realize that *Tylecodon* is an anagram of its former generic name. There was a reason why this group of plants was separated: cotyledons proper are not deciduous, rarely losing all their leaves according to the seasons but retaining them to help the plants through hard times. Tylecodons on the other hand have caudices (thickened tree-like stems), are deciduous and come into growth only when the conditions are right – when the rains come. They prefer to conserve their energies during droughts by shedding their leaves and not losing moisture through them.

There are about 30 species in this genus, coming from the winter rainfall areas of West Cape Province in South Africa and Namibia. These plants grow and flower in the winter months in the northern hemisphere and need a minimum temperature of 5°C (41°F). They like a well-drained soil, although are not too fussy.

Some of the species are quite tiny: *Tylecodon schaeferianus* reaches only 15 cm (6 in) in height. Others, such as *T. paniculatus*, can reach a height of 1.5 m (5 ft) in the wild, so it is important to select the species to suit your conditions.

The smaller growing species include *T. bucholzianus*, very slow growing, clumping readily and resembling a small group of brown corals when resting and without leaves; *T. schaeferianus* (syn. *T. sinus-alexandri*), with white or pink flowers, and small, roundish leaves, rather loosely attached.

The larger growing species include *T. cacalioides*, a tree reaching heights of 1 m (3 ft); *T. paniculatus*, a tree to 1.5 m (5 ft) high and 60 cm (2 ft) in diameter; *T. reticulatus*, a tree growing to 1.75 m (5¾ ft) high, looking as though it is festooned on top with barbed wire when it flowers; and *T. wallichii*, tree-like, attaining 1 m (3 ft) in height.

Above: ***Yucca filamentosa*****, in its variegated form, is one of the more commonly found garden species**

Yucca (Agavaceae)

Yuccas, like agaves, come from the Americas. They can sometimes be relatively small – *Yucca endlichiana* has leaves that come from ground level and are about 30 cm (12 in) tall – to the giant *Y. brevifolia* (Joshua tree), which attains a height of 7.5 m (25 ft) with age and can be quite a size across having many heads. Neither of these species will do well in gardens in temperate areas because of the moisture.

Y. elata is frequently sold as a houseplant. It is also sold as a small section of stem or a little 'log', which is sealed with wax at both ends to conserve moisture. Rarely does this piece of wood fail to root, so tenacious is the plant in its desire to live. As a houseplant it will soon outgrow its welcome. With age the plant base thickens considerably and gets to the point where it is difficult to find a pot in which to plant it on. It will also, if kept long enough, get too tall for the average room. Eventually such plants tend to be left outside for the winter and therefore die.

The species that are most often seen in garden centres, and hence gardens, are *Y. gloriosa*, *Y. flaccida* and *Y. filamentosa*. The first two species will make large clumps or bushes, multiplying after flowering. *Y. gloriosa* will also sucker from underground. These plants are not particularly fussy about the type of soil that they grow in, but *Y. gloriosa* has been known to rot at the base if it is kept too wet. Make sure that leaf debris is kept away from the base of the plant to avoid this. *Y. filamentosa* is available as a plain green-leaved variety or, more interestingly, as a variegated form, such as 'Variegata'. These three species will do very well in mild, temperate areas, especially in chalky soil.

It is probable that many more species would be able to withstand frost and snow, but so far the range available at garden centres is limited. Perhaps an enterprising nurseryman will experiment with some other species, now that global warming is giving drier summers and milder winters.

In the greenhouse or conservatory the following species can be easily accommodated: *Y. glauca*, *Y. endlichiana*, *Y. carnerosana*, *Y. whipplei*, *Y. harrimaniae* and *Y. baccata*. *Y. glauca* and *Y. whipplei* should be hardy, and if these are grown from seed it would be worthwhile experimenting with the odd seedling to test its hardiness. All yucca plants benefit from being out of doors for the summer months.

All of these plants will flower, perhaps not every year but most years. The flowers are usually cream-white with occasional hints of pink. They are borne on tall stems and are roughly bell-shaped and usually pendent, although in some species the flowers are upright against the stem. They are rich in nectar and, when grown in the open, may attract aphids which in turn attract ants.

A word of caution about the leaves on these plants. The species that have rigid leaves usually also have a very sharp tip on the end. Wherever they are grown, it is important to keep these plants towards the back of the border or staging.

Equipment, Bibliography and Glossary

Equipment

Having the right tools to hand will make looking after your cacti and succulents easier.

Knives A selection of sharp, clean knives for taking cuttings is useful.
Labels and pens Make sure your plants are labelled with a light-fast and waterproof pen and record as much data as possible.
Maximum/minimum thermometer
For a greenhouse or conservatory or a windowsill collection.
Mister A small hand-held mister is useful for mixing up insecticides and zapping pests. They are also useful for damping down on hot days.
Polystyrene tiles Probably the worst problem is how to handle spiny plants without damaging yourself or the plants. Having something to tip the plants onto helps. Ceiling or flooring tiles are cheap, rigid and can be washed off easily.
Stakes Really large plants need some form of support, particularly if they are going to be transported. Some cacti do not make much of a woody core and easily snap off.
Supports For clambering plants, trellis supports and plastic-covered ties are often needed.
Tweezers Grasping hold of pots can be tricky. Heavy duty tweezers or grabbers will be useful not only for handling pots but also for handling cuttings of taller plants. Smaller tweezers are good for pulling spines out of hands, etc.
Watering can A can with a long reach spout and a fine rose is ideal. A smaller version will help you to deliver the correct amount of water to a plant.

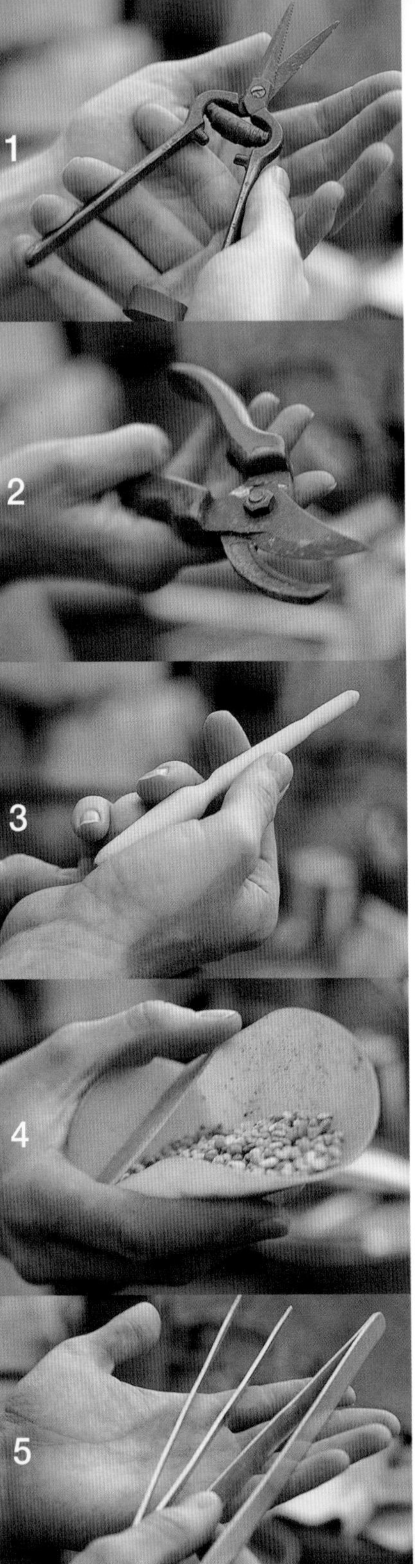

Right: 1. A pair of grape vine secateurs with very fine blades, ideal for taking small cuttings **2.** Secateurs for taking larger cuttings **3.** Dibber for planting out small seedlings or cuttings **4.** Plastic scoop for putting soil around a plant or for top dressing with small gravel **5.** Large tweezers for grabbing spiny plants

Bibliography

The following is a list of helpful cactus and succulent literature. The list is by no means exhaustive as it does not contain many Floras that have been published on particular areas where succulent plants are found:

Anderson, E. F., *Peyote: The Divine Cactus*, University of Arizona Press, 1996 ISBN 0 8165 1653 7

Anderson, E. F., Montes, S.A., Taylor, N.P., *Threatened Cacti of Mexico*, Royal Botanic Gardens Kew, 1994 ISBN 0 947643 69 9

Backeberg, C., *Cactus Lexicon*, Blandford Press, 1966 ISBN 0 7137 0840 9

Bally, P. R. O., *The Genus Monadenium*, Benteli Publishers, Berne, 1961

Bayer, M. B., *The New Haworthia Handbook*, National Botanic Gardens of South Africa, 1982 ISBN 0 620 05632 0

Benson, L., *The Cacti of the United States and Canada*, Stanford University Press, 1982 ISBN 0 8047 0863 0

Borg, J., *Cacti*, Blandford Press, Third Edition, 1959.

Bregman, R., *The Genus Matucana*, A. A. Balkema, 1996 ISBN 90 5410 638 7

Britton, N. L. and Rose, J. N., *The Cactaceae*, The Carnegie Institute of Washington, 1919

Buining, A. F. H., *Discocactus, Succulenta*

Buxbaum, F., *Cactus Culture Based on Biology*, Blandford Press, 1958

Buxbaum, F., *Morphology of Cacti*, Abbey Garden Press, 1959

Cole, D.T., *Lithops: Flowering Stones*, Russel Friedman Books, 1988 ISBN 0 620 09678 0

Cullmann, W., Götz, E., and Gröner, G., *The Encyclopedia of Cacti*, Alphabooks, 1984 ISBN 0 906670 37 3

Dyer, R. A., *Ceropegia, Brachystelma and Riocreuxia in Southern Africa*, A. A. Balkema, 1983 ISBN 90 6191 227 X

Eggli, U., *Glossary of Botanical Terms with special reference to Succulent Plants*, The British Cactus and Succulent Society, 1993 ISBN 0 902099 22 1

Eggli, U., *Sukkulenten*, Eugen Ulmer, 1994 ISBN 3 8001 6512 0

Gentry, H. S., *Agaves of Continental North America*, University of Arizona Press, 1982 ISBN 0 8165 0775 9

Hammer, S.A., *The Genus Conophytum: A Conograph*, Succulent Plant Publications, Pretoria, 1993 ISBN 0 620 17634 2

Hewitt, T., *The Complete Book of Cacti & Succulents*, Dorling Kindersley, 1993 ISBN 0 7513 0049 7

Higgins, V., *Crassulas in Cultivation*, Blandford Press, 1964

Hodoba, T. B., *Growing Desert Plants: from Windowsill to Garden*, Red Crane Books, 1995 ISBN 1 878610 54 6

Jacobsen, H., *A Handbook of Succulent Plants*, Blandford Press, 1960.

Jacobsen, H., *Lexicon of Succulent Plants*, Blandford Press, 1974 ISBN 07137 0652 X

Lawrie, I., *Coryphantha and Associated Genera*, The Mammillaria Society, 1988

Mace, T., *Notocactus*, National Cactus and Succulent Society, Sussex Zone, 1975

MacMillan, A. J. S., and Horobin, J. F., *Christmas Cacti: The Genus Schlumbergera and its Hybrids*, 1995, David Hunt ISBN 0 9517234 6 4

Nel, G. C., *The Gibbaeum Handbook*, Blandford Press, 1953

Nobel, P. S., *The Environmental Biology of Agaves and Cacti*, Cambridge University Press, 1988 ISBN 0 521 34322 4

Pilbeam, J., *Mammillaria: A Collectors' Guide*, B. T. Batsford Ltd, 1981 ISBN 0 7134 3987 5

Pilbeam, J., *Sulcorebutia and Weingartia: A Collectors' Guide*, B. T. Batsford Ltd, 1985 ISBN 0 7134 4672 2

Pilbeam, J., *Thelocactus*, Cirio Publishing Services Ltd., 1996 ISBN 0 9528302 0 5

Rauh, W., *Succulent and Xerophytic Plants of Madagascar* (Vol 1), Strawberry Press, 1995 ISBN 0 912647 14 0

Rausch, W., *Lobivia,* W. Rausch, 1975

Rowley, G. D., *Anacampseros, Avonia, Grahamia*, The British Cactus and Succulent Society, 1995 ISBN 0 902099 29 9

Rowley, G. D., *A History of Succulent Plants*, Strawberry Press, 1997 ISBN 0 912647 16 0

Rowley, G. D., *Caudiciform and Pachycaul Succulents*, Strawberry Press, 1987 ISBN 0 912647 03 5

Rowley, G. D., *Didiereaceae: 'Cacti of the Old World'*, The British Cactus and Succulent Society, 1992 ISBN 0 902099 20 5

Rowley, G. D., *Name that Succulent*, Stanley Thornes (Publishers) Ltd., 1980 ISBN 0 85950 447 6

Rowley, G. D., *Succulent Compositae*, Strawberry Press, 1994 ISBN 0 912647 12 4

Rowley, G. D., *The Adenium and Pachypodium Handbook*, The British Cactus and Succulent Society, 1983 ISBN 0 902099 07 8

Reynolds, G. W., *The Aloes of South Africa*, A. A. Balkema, 1974 ISBN 0 86961 064 3

Reynolds, G. W., *The Aloes of Tropical Africa and Madagascar*, The Aloes Book Fund, 1966

Schwantes, G., *The Cultivation of the Mesembryanthemaceae*, Blandford Press, 1954

Schulz, R. and Kapitany, A., *Copiapoa in their Environment*, Published by the authors, 1996

Schwartz *et al.*, H., *The Euphorbia Journal*, Vols 1–10, Strawberry Press, 1983–1997

Spain, J., *Growing Winter Hardy Cacti*, 1994

Stephenson, R., *Sedum: Cultivated Stonecrops*, Timber Press Inc., 1994 ISBN 0 88192 238 2

Storms, E., *The New Growing the Mesembs*, Ed Storms Inc., 1986

van Jaarsveld, E., *Gasterias of Southern Africa*, Fernwood Press, 1994 ISBN 1 874950 01 6

Walther, E., *Echeveria*, California Academy of Sciences, 1972

White A., and Sloane, B. L., *The Stapelieae*, Abbey San Encino Press, 1937

Zappi, D. C., *Pilosocereus (Cactaceae): The Genus in Brazil*, David Hunt, 1994, ISBN 0 9517234 4 8

Glossary

Adventitious Part of a plant that appears in an unusual or unexpected place, such as roots on stems or plantlets on leaves.

Areole The cushion of spines, almost always with fine hairs, which is characteristic of cacti. They represent short, modified shoots.

Axil The angle between the stem and a leaf, also the region at the base of and between the tubercles. Hairs, bristles, side shoots or flowers may be produced at the axils.

Bract A modified leaf at the base of a flower.

Caudex The massively enlarged portion of stems and sometimes roots often of a succulent nature.

Cephalium A distinctly separate region of certain cactus species, usually with densely bristly or woolly areoles, from which the flowers are produced.

Chlorosis A more or less distinct lack of chlorophyll leading to the plant having a sickly yellow colour. Often a symptom of deficiency of a micro-nutrient such as iron or boron.

Cristate Having abnormal fasciated or fan-like growth due to an elongated instead of point-like growing point.

Deltoid Shaped like the Greek letter D (Delta).

Dichotomous With two equal or similar choices, branched in two with two equal branches, forked.

Ephemeral Short lived.

Epicuticular Growing or developing on the cuticle of a plant.

Epiphytic Growing on other plants, but not parasitic on them.

Etiolated A type of abnormally elongated growth, paler green due to a partial lack of chlorophyll because of insufficient light.

Excrescence Outgrowth, warty appendage, protuberance.

Farina A flour-like, mealy white powder.

Fasciated Having abnormal growth with flattened and laterally expanded stems, or irregular stems; caused by abnormal divisions of the growing point.

Fissure The aperture between two otherwise united leaves.

Glaucous Covered with a greyish-white or bluish-white/green bloom.

Glochids Very fine spines covered with microscopically small barbs, and typical of the Opuntioideae sub-family.

Glutinous Sticky, glue-like.

Hydroponics The practice of growing plants in a nutrient solution instead of in soil.

Hygrochastic Moving of plant parts caused by absorbing water or drying out.

Inflorescence A plant branch which carries the flowers.

Keeled Having a raised ridge, like the keel of a ship.

Lanceolate Shaped like a lance.

Lath house A structure made of narrow wooden slats that reduces the power of the sun and affords protection against the wind and slight frost.

Monocarpic Flowering once at the end of a life span and then dying after the fruits have ripened.

Ovary The bottom part of the cactus flower with an internal cavity containing the ovules.

Peduncle The main stalk of a whole inflorescence.

Photosynthesis A physiological process carried out by green plants in which solar energy is used to convert carbon dioxide and water into sugars (food) with the help of chlorophyll.

Pruinose Covered with a fine, whitish, slightly powdery layer like a plum (due to a fine layer of epicuticular wax).

Pubescent Having short hairs or down.

Retuse Notched at the apex of the leaf or petal.

Ribs Parts of the body of a cactus forming raised ridges running more or less vertically.

Scales External structures, often formed on the ovary and the tube of cactus flowers.

Scion The upper part of a graft– i.e., the piece grafted on to a more robust grafting stock.

Serrated With saw-like teeth.

Spathulate Spatula shaped, i.e. tapering from a rounded apex into a gradually narrowing stalk.

Spines In the botanical sense superficial growths on the stems or leaves, as opposed to thorns, which are modified leaves or stems. The spines of cacti should really be termed thorns, as they are modified leaves.

Succulent Thick-fleshed and capable of storing large quantities of water.

Tube The humps, or warts, which occur on the stems of many cacti and which bear areoles. In some cacti such as *Mammillaria*, the tubercles are the remains of ribs which have become deeply notched.

Tubercles An underground fleshy stem or stem segment with several buds, e.g. a potato; or a fleshy root or root part.

Vascular bundle A bundle of tissue consisting of elongated cells which serve to transport water and food. In succulent dicotyledons these can be seen as an annular arrangement of fine threads in the cross-section of the stem.

Viscid Sticky, glutinous.

Xerophyte Any plant showing some degree of adaption to environments with very little precipitation.

Zygomorphic flowers Bilaterally symmetrical flowers as opposed to flowers with full circular symmetry.

Index

Figures in *italics* indicate pictures.

Photographic acknowledgements

Octopus Publishing Group Limited/Jerry Harpur 61 top right, 61 bottom left, 66, 67, 68 bottom left, 73 bottom right, 74 bottom right, 77 top left/Peter Myers 1, 4–5, 10–11, 15 top right, 16 top right, 21, 22, 23, 25, 26 top left, 26 bottom left, 27 left, 27 right, 27 bottom right, 28, 30, 32, 33, 34–35, 36, 38, 40–41, 43, 44, 45, 46, 48, 51, 52–53, 54, 55, 56 top left, 56 bottom right, 57, 58, 59, 62, 63, 64 top right, 64 bottom left, 68 top right, 70, 71, 74 top left, 75, 76, 77 bottom right, 78, 79, 80, 81, 82 top right, 82 bottom left, 83 top right, 83 bottom left, 84 top left, 85, 86 top right, 86 bottom left, 87, 88 top left, 88 bottom right, 90, 92, 93, 94, 95, 96, 97, 98, 100 top left, 100 bottom right, 101, 102 top left, 102 bottom right, 103, 104, 105, 106, 107, 108, 109, 111, 112, 114, 115, 120 top right, 120 centre right, 120 bottom right, 120 bottom centre right, 120 top centre right/James Young 2–3, 6–7, 17, 72, 73 top left, 84 bottom right, 117, 118–119.
Tony Mace 9, 15 bottom left, 16 bottom left, 18–19, 37, 50, 60, 65, 91.

Publisher's acknowledgements

Executive Editor Sarah Ford
Project Editor Leanne Bryan
Executive Art Editor Geoff Fennell
Designer Janis Utton
Illustration Fiona Fraser
Senior Production Controller Martin Croshaw
Assistant Picture Librarian Taura Riley